To Richard

# Dancing In The Chequered Shade

*Poetry in a Difficult Year*

Frances Thomas

Published 2017 by arima publishing
www.arimapublishing.com

ISBN 978 1 84549 722 4

© Frances Thomas 2017

All rights reserved

This book is copyright. Subject to statutory exception and to provisions of relevant collective licensing agreements, no part of this publication may be reproduced, stored in a retrieval system, or transmitted in any form or by any means, without the prior written permission of the author.

Printed and bound in the United Kingdom

Typeset in Garamond

This book is sold subject to the conditions that it shall not, by way of trade or otherwise, be lent, re-sold, hired out, or otherwise circulated without the publisher's prior consent in any form of binding or cover other than that which it is published and without a similar condition including this condition being imposed on the subsequent purchaser.

The author has made every attempt to ensure that no copyright has been breached. Any problems can be rectified in any future edition

arima publishing

ASK House, Northgate Avenue
Bury St Edmunds, Suffolk IP32 6BB
t: (+44) 01284 700321
www.arimapublishing.com

# Introduction – January 2016

People will often tell you they have no time for poetry, as though it's something that keeps them from the really important things in their lives. Yet when they marry, they want to count the ways, when they die, to stop all the clocks. They turn, in fact, to poetry. Every time the words of a song go round and round in your brain, or a rhyme you knew as a child jumps up in your mind, it's poetry that's getting to you. A beautiful piece of Shakespeare might haunt you: Tennyson's favourite line of Shakespeare's was the eerily beautiful *Hang there, like fruit, my soul, till the tree die,* from Cymbeline. The writer Frances Towers was obsessed by a line from *Midsummer Night's Dream* which I must have read many times without properly seeing it: *Turns into yellow gold his salt green streams.* Donne's line *A bracelet of bright hair about the bone* always makes my hair stand up. Or something far more commonplace – I can't sit on a train hurtling through the countryside without *Faster than fairies, faster than witches* running on a tape-loop through my brain.

A few years ago, it occurred to me that I wasn't reading nearly enough poetry on a daily basis. I'd got out of the habit, for all the lazy reasons one gets out of good habits and into bad. So I made a resolution that I'd try to read a different poem every day, for a year. It wasn't intended to turn into a journal, still less into a book, but somehow it did both.

I called it *A Bracelet of Bright Hair* and it was a record of my poetry reading over the year. I chose poems that suited whatever was going on that day, or sometimes I just chose a poem I liked. It turned into a poetry diary, and I finished the year determined to keep up my habit of closely reading a poem a day. I didn't, of course, bad habits come back quickly, but I have tried to read more poetry since then.

When I wrote that book in 2010 it was a quiet year; but since then, the world has become a much nastier place; initial euphoria over the fall of tyrants turning to despair as countries descend into chaos, and the unspeakable Isis, with its bizarre concept of paradise as a kind of brothel pimped by God, floods the world with hate and murder. And the problem of how to deal with all the people displaced by this brutality has become the humanitarian crisis of our age. Ancient buildings are being torn down, and treasures destroyed. Global warming and climate change have become tangible, the headlong rush of greed and destruction seems unstoppable; icebergs melt, rain-forests burn, deserts spread. (And in addition to all of this, there now seems a real threat that Donald Trump might become President of the United States; it would be like a Hanna and Barbera cartoon if it weren't so frightening.)

And on a personal level, our own lives have been turned upside down. In 2013, Richard, my husband, suffered a major heart attack while dropping a friend off at Birmingham airport. Miraculously he survived – if you have to have a heart attack, an airport is quite a good place to do so, with defibrillators on call, and a passing plastic surgeon, who had just recently attended a refresher course in resuscitation. Richard is now fitted up with stents and his own state-of-the-art defibrillator and seems to be doing well. But then a few months later, obviously jealous of all the attention he was getting, I was diagnosed with myeloma, a blood-and-bone cancer. Since that time, our lives have been a network of hospital appointments, pills and medical regimes. I'm in quite good shape at the moment, though running at half-power. But it's strange not to be the person I was just a few years ago – I used to spend mornings doing the garden, clambering up hills, striding through London streets. I used to jump on and off trains and buses, lugging my suitcase; I used to go up stairs two at a time. I've climbed rocky hills in Egypt and Greece without thinking twice. I could spend a day with my granddaughter without getting tired. I prided myself on never getting ill. Now all that's changed. I miss myself. I don't much like this new person they've given me, but I am having to learn to get along with her.

So why am I starting this project again after five years? Well, partly because I enjoyed compiling the first one so much – looking at poems each day, enjoying the magical moments when a poem that was just right appeared from nowhere, or leafing through favourite poets, or discovering new ones, that I just wanted to enjoy the experience again. I found it shaped each day and gave the days a purpose. Being ill has something to do with it too; embarking on a project that should if completed take me through till the end of the year is rather like cocking a snook at the Grim Reaper. If I make it through to the end of the year, that's to be celebrated, if not, well it could always be made into a good sales pitch for the book. Cancer diaries seem to be all the rage at the moment, though, and in spite of the way this one starts, I hope my year will be memorable for things other than illness. I've chosen some lovely poems, by the best poets, and occasionally a suitable piece of prose; but also I've had the temerity to insert a few that I wrote myself. Usually I express myself in prose, but just sometimes there's a moment, or an impulse, where only a poem will do, and so I've had to try and grapple with that impulse with a poem of my own.

(January 2017 – This stays as I wrote it at the time – oh how I wish I'd been wrong about Donald Trump.)

# *January*

## January 5th

My year has begun several days into January; Christmas and the New Year found me laid low with a chest infection, and when it didn't clear, I ended up in hospital, attached to several drips. It's an odd experience being in hospital; I've never had so much care and attention in my life; my temperature, my blood, (or my 'bloods' as medics oddly call them) my blood pressure, are all monitored in the minutest degree, nurses and doctors hover over me, ask me questions and listen most carefully to the answers. I've become a different person, I'm the lady in the bed by the door, a clutch of statistics on a clipboard, I'm 'sweetheart' and 'love' and 'darling' (Yes, I could ask them not to call me that; but on the whole, it's done so sweetly, it seems mean to object.). But it's as though a cartoon double of myself has slipped free of my old self and is existing in some strange dimension beyond my control.

Still, I did make up a poem in the hospital; and here it is.

## Blackbird

That blackbird sending bubbles of sound into the sky,
doesn't know he sings outside the cancer ward,
the garden built by kind hands so patients can
touch leaves and smell roses.
But now in January, rain drips from massed bamboos
and the roses are a crown of thorns.

In the corridors machines, those bossy guardians, bleep and chirrup,
and pale bald women stand like candles.
They will not die today, nor tomorrow,
but they know they might not see the roses.

They'd like to be themselves, but their lives
are stored away in files; they've become
their blood, their sputum, their pee, their tears.

They miss themselves; they know they're waiting somewhere
in another world, not far, but out of reach,
They have nowhere else to go, no-one else to be, while the wait goes on.

The blackbird of course knows nothing about this,
and wouldn't care if he did. His concerns
are both more ancient and more new,
but he knows he has to sing
and keep singing
into that cold sky.

## January 12th

Back in the outside world, which has turned into a world of rain, dripping down day after day, night after night, from a grey sodden sky. Fields by the side of the road have turned into lakes stretching silvery smooth as far as you can see, new waterfalls tumble excitedly from rocks and sweep across the road in huge puddles, the grass has turned into a sort of sodden sponge, with little nourishment in it for the anxiously chomping sheep.

Here's an enigmatic poem by Edward Thomas, which he wrote in the last year of his life, remembering an earlier occasion when he'd been caught in a downpour, but putting into it all his feelings of dejection and despair; feeling both a premonition of his own death, and a bond of sympathy with those who aren't going to die, but will feel the sadness of the rain and the sadness of death.

A couple of years ago, we went with friends to visit Edward Thomas's grave at Agny cemetery near Arras. We drove through that strange section of Northern France where none of the buildings is old. We enjoyed Arras, its grey houses ranged in severely beautiful squares. Agny was a small, unremarkable village, and the cemetery lay at the end of it. We went down a narrow suburban path, through hedges and neat vegetable gardens, into the cemetery, beautifully kept of course. By World War One standards it was a small one, only 408 British graves, and five German. All the graves told their little dramas, all terribly sad.

We found Edward Thomas's grave, and wished we'd had a flower to lay on it, but there were no flower shops in the seaside town where we were staying. His devoted wife Helen believed that he'd died without a mark on his body, killed by a shell passing just by him, but a recent biography reveals that this wasn't true; he died from a bullet in the chest. Not that the manner of his death matters; he's still just one of those 400 graves, but at least his poetry survives him.

## Rain – Edward Thomas

Rain, midnight rain, nothing but the wild rain
On this bleak hut, and solitude, and me
Remembering again that I shall die
And neither hear the rain nor give it thanks
For washing me cleaner than I have been
Since I was born into this solitude.
Blessed are the dead that the rain rains upon:
But here I pray that none whom once I loved
Is dying to-night or lying still awake

Solitary, listening to the rain,
Either in pain or thus in sympathy
Helpless among the living and the dead,
Like a cold water among broken reeds,
Myriads of broken reeds all still and stiff,
Like me who have no love which this wild rain
Has not dissolved except the love of death,
If love it be towards what is perfect and
Cannot, the tempest tells me, disappoint.

## January 20th

For the first time this year, a stunningly beautiful day – a shaft of sunlight stains the bracken-topped hill a deep crimson, while hedgerows and tree-tops shimmer under a silvery hoar-front. The beautiful day is followed by a fantastic night, a nearly full moon and a dazzling spatter of stars. And in the world of science, there's excited talk of a new planet, way beyond the visible ones of our solar system, trackable only by distortions in space. This planet might be many times the size of our earth and take 2,000 years to travel round the sun. A friend has posted this poem on Facebook.

### The Undiscovered Planet – Norman Nicholson

Out on the furthest tether let it run
Its hundred-year-long-orbit, cold
As solid mercury, old and dead
Before this world's fermenting bread
Had got a crust to cover it; landscape of lead
Whose purple voes and valleys are
Lit faintly by a sun
No nearer than a measurable star.

No man has seen it, nor the lensed eye
That pin-points week by week the same patch of sky
Records even a blue across its pupil. Only
The errantry of Saturn, the wry
Retarding of Uranus, speak
Of the pull beyond the pattern.
The unknown is shown
Only by a bend in the known.

## January 23rd

Burns Night, and like many non-Scots, I can't quite see the point of Robert Burns; he was obviously a charismatic character, but a drunk and – like Byron, whose birthday it was yesterday – beastly to women. Like Byron he was a romantic radical, though he'd planned at one time to work on a slave plantation in Jamaica. Much of his poetry leaves me cold, but he did write a handful of beautiful love lyrics like this one. Though while he was courting Nancy, he was still married to Jean, and busy seducing Jenny and Margaret. Nancy did well to get out.

### Ae Fond Kiss – Robert Burns
Ae fond kiss, and then we sever;
Ae fareweel, alas, for ever!
Deep in heart-wrung tears I'll pledge thee,
Warring sighs and groans I'll wage thee!
Who shall say that Fortune grieves him
While the star of hope she leaves him?
Me, nae cheerfu' twinkle lights me,
Dark despair around benights me.

I'll ne'er blame my partial fancy;
Naething could resist my Nancy;
For to see her was to love her,
Love but her, and love for ever.
Had we never loved sae kindly,
Had we never loved sae blindly,
Never met—or never parted,
We had ne'er been broken-hearted.
Fare thee weel, thou first and fairest!
Fare thee weel, thou best and dearest!
Thine be ilka joy and treasure,
Peace, enjoyment, love, and pleasure!
Ae fond kiss, and then we sever!
Ae fareweel, alas, for ever!
Deep in heart-wrung tears I'll pledge thee,
Warring sighs and groans I'll wage thee

## January 27th

It's Holocaust Memorial Day today, so impossible to think of anything trivial. Still, I can't ignore it, and the images it conjures up. I was born in 1943, too young to remember the war, but I can't remember when I first heard about the Holocaust. It wasn't part of the war stories and memories that we heard constantly. My grandmother didn't like Jews and would say so, but then she didn't like anybody, so I never counted her dislikes as meaning anything. I had a Jewish friend, Patsy, at my primary school (No, my grandmother didn't like her; said she had a dirty vest) and one day when I went home with her, I remember her father telling me, kindly and gently, about the persecution that Jews suffered. I don't expect he ever remembered that he'd said those things to me, but I never forgot them; he laid down something crucial in my mind, and I've always been grateful to him; people aren't always aware of the importance things they've said or done can have for others. My next contact with Jews came much later – a couple called Joe and Roz moved into our dull suburban street. She was New York, he was London. They were colourful, exotic, even tolerant of my antisemitic grandmother. Though not religious – they were raging communists – they were enmeshed in Jewish culture and Jewish ways. I remember babysitting for them, reading *Russia Today* and *China Reconstructs*. They also changed my young life, and reminded me of the crass stupidity and wickedness of judging a religion or a nation through hate and prejudice.

Now we are seeing images everyday on the news, of families displaced through fear and violence – refugees living in unimaginable misery in makeshift tents amidst winter cold and rain. It's easy to consider them as though we're peering through a dingy window – something terrible is going on, but it's not happening to us. But the most vivid description I know of what it actually feels like to be uprooted from your home and sent off in squalor to an unknown fate comes (probably) from Shakespeare, 500 years ago.

The play is *Sir Thomas More*, a composite effort by Antony Munday and Henry Chettle, but most famous for an insert of three pages in manuscript, in an unknown hand, called 'Hand D', and now believed to be that of Shakespeare. More is addressing a riotous crowd which wants to drive out all the immigrants in the city, and he tries to make people feel exactly what it must be like to be displaced and landless. You are taken into the consciousness of those comfortable families in Vienna in the Thirties, or in Damascus in our own time, with lives suddenly shattered, and imagine what it must feel like to be wrenched away from your familiar life, leaving behind everything you own except what you can carry, and to travel, with family members, young, old or sick, unable to succour them, through danger and filth to an alien country where you're probably going to encounter as much hostility as you've left behind. Put yourself in those people's shoes, More says eloquently, and try to feel their feelings; and then imagine it happening to you.

### *From* Sir Thomas More – (probably) Shakespeare

Grant them removed, and grant that this your noise
Hath chid down all the majesty of England;
Imagine that you see the wretched strangers,
Their babies at their backs and their poor luggage,
Plodding to the ports and coasts for transportation,
And that you sit as kings in your desires,
Authority quite silent by your brawl,
And you in ruff of your opinions clothed;
What had you got? I'll tell you. You had taught
How insolence and strong hand should prevail,
How order should be quelled; and by this pattern
Not one of you should live an aged man,
For other ruffians, as their fancies wrought,
With self same hand, self reasons, and self right,
Would shark on you, and men like ravenous fishes
Would feed on one another.
Say now the king
Should so much come too short of your great trespass
As but to banish you, whither would you go?
What country, by the nature of your error,
Should give you harbour? Go you to France or Flanders,
To any German province, to Spain or Portugal,
Nay anywhere that not adheres to England,

Why you must needs be strangers; would you be pleased
To find a nation of such barbarous temper
That breaking out in hideous violence
Would not afford you an abode on earth,
Whet their detested knives against your throats,
Spurn you like dogs, and like as if that God
Owed not nor made not you, nor that the claimants
Were not at all appropriate to your comforts
But chartered unto them, what would you think
To be thus used? This is the strangers case
And this your mountainish inhumanity.

## January 28th

Although it's still dank and gloomy, there are signs that spring is on its way; the days are getting longer, primroses star the hedgerows and daffodils have fat yellow buds. It's been an unusually mild winter, so everything is earlier than usual, which is why this poem of Hardy's, though it talks of March, seems to fit the mood of this dark and muggy late January day. He describes that mysterious and beautiful moment after the winter when, as though a switch has suddenly been turned on, spring starts to happen.

## The Year's Awakening – Thomas Hardy

How do you know that the pilgrim track
Along the belting zodiac
Swept by the sun in his seeming rounds
Is traced by now to the Fishes' bounds
And into the Ram, when weeks of cloud
Have wrapt the sky in a clammy shroud,
And never as yet a tinct of spring

Has shown in the earth's apparelling;
Oh vespering bird, how do you know,
How do you know?
How do you know deep underground
Hid in your bed from sight and sound,
Without a turn in temperature,
With weather life can scarce endure,
That light has won a fraction's strength,
And day put on some moment's length,
Whereof in merest rote will come,
Weeks hence, mild airs that do not numb;
O crocus root, how do you know,
How do you know?

## January 29th

This, although it's a children's poem, I include because it's been running through my head all night, a simpler version on the same theme as Hardy's poem. I remember it from infant school, where somebody must have read it to us. I associate it with sitting, bare-kneed and long-socked, on the dusty floor of the assembly hall; I can smell that floor as I sit here now, and the plasticine smell of other children and cabbagey school dinners. There was a picture on the wall which haunted me – it showed a sad old man in a surplice walking through a park with other men. I knew that something terrible was about to happen. But I'd got it wrong – the man walking behind the sad old man wore a great black hat with a feather and a fine jacket; and it was he, Charles I, walking to his execution, to whom the terrible event was to happen, not the old archbishop.

Listening to that poem, I pictured the tiny seeds stirring deep in the earth, and felt the excitement of their awakening. Now I could only remember the first two lines of the poem, but looking it up now, I find to my surprise that Google remembers it too, and with more surprise, that it was by E. Nesbit. And actually, it is rather charming.

**Baby Seed Song – Edith Nesbit**
Little brown brother, oh! little brown brother,
Are you awake in the dark?
Here we lie cosily, close to each other:
Hark to the song of the lark
"Waken!" the lark says, "waken and dress you;
Put on your green coats and gay,
Blue sky will shine on you, sunshine caress you
Waken! 'tis morning 'tis May!"
Little brown brother, oh! little brown brother,
What kind of a flower will you be?
I'll be a poppy all white, like my mother;
Do be a poppy like me.
What! You're a sunflower! How I shall miss you
When you're grown golden and high!
But I shall send all the bees up to kiss you;
Little brown brother, good-bye.

**January 30th**
We take the opportunity, during a brief patch of polished blue sky and sunlight, to go for a drive over the military range of the Epynt, which usually we have to ourselves. Today, though, we're stopped by a hunt gathering, jeeps and range rovers and horse boxes, and

jaunty riders on restless and high stepping horses, blocking the road and with all the entitlement of such groups, not imagining that we might actually be wanting to pass rather than follow them. So we have to trail them at a snail's pace, and actually, with horses and the snuffling hounds and the riding habits and helmets, they make quite a decorative scene, in spite of the cruelty of the sport in which they're indulging. I remember another poem from school, this time about ten years later; I'm sitting at my desk with my brown-paper bound copy of that year's poetry anthology, and I'm reading this, by John Masefield. I'm not sentimental about foxes, having picked up the remnants of our own chicken flock from a released urban fox one cold Christmas Day years ago (the fox was shot by a farmer almost immediately afterwards – urban foxes don't have the skills to survive in the wild; it's cruel to release them in the country). But I don't think watching them torn to pieces is something that civilised people should enjoy. Although in this long poem, Masefield is celebrating the world of the Hunt, he does at least allow the fox to get away in the end. It's hard to think, though, that someone could write this and still be supportive of hunting.

### *From* Reynard The Fox – John Masefield
The fox was strong, he was full of running,
He could run for an hour and then be cunning,
But the cry behind him made him chill,
They were nearer now and they meant to kill,
They meant to run him till his blood
Clogged on his heart as his brush with mud,
Till his back bent up and his tongue hung flagging,
And his belly and brush were filthed from dragging,
Till he crouched stone still, dead beat and dirty,
With nothing but teeth against the thirty,

And all the way to that blundering end
He would meet with men and have none his friend,
Men to holla and men to run him,
With stones to stagger and yells to stun him,
Men to head him, with whips to beat him,
Teeth to mangle and mouths to eat him,
And all the way that high weird crying
To cold his blood with the thought of dying…

## January 31$^{st}$

This poem, from an American friend who was celebrating her fortieth wedding anniversary, landed in my mailbox this morning. I wrote a biography of Christina Rossetti some years ago, so I ought to feel I know her well, but I don't, and I don't think anyone did. She wrote many passionate poems about love, and we can surmise that she was deeply in love at least a couple of times in her life, but as her life went on, religion, always a powerful force for her, overwhelmed her more and more, and this poem from her middle years is about the transcendental and perfect love she believes she will encounter from God when at last she enters Heaven.

## At Last – Christina Rossetti

Many have sung of love a root of bane
    When to my mind a root of balm it is,
    For love at length breeds love; sufficient bliss
For life and death and rising up again.
Surely when light of Heaven makes all things plain,
    Love will grow plain with all its mysteries,
    Nor shall we need to fetch from over seas
Wisdom or wealth or pleasure safe from pain.

Love in our borders, love within our heart,
    Love all in all, we then shall bide at rest,
    Ended forever life's unending quest,
Ended for ever effort, change and fear,
Love all in all; no more that better part
    Purchased, but at the cost of all things here.

# February

## February 3rd

Feeling a bit grey on a grey day this morning; partly because it's February, never my favourite month of the year, and partly because I'm still shaking off my second nasty cold of the year (picked up from talking to a class of nice schoolchildren last week – a hazard of having a rubbish immune system, and already passed on to Richard, who doesn't need bad colds either.) I feel I need something simply beautiful to put in my poetry year, and it reminded me of another grey day, a year or so ago, when I was waiting, with a painful cracked back, in the lovely Maggie's Centre in Cheltenham for radiotherapy treatment in the hospital that afternoon. I dozed in a comfortable chair, and found – unlike the usual shelf-rubbish – some decent books, including a collected edition of Yeats. There I found my simply beautiful poem, and here it is.

## The Wild Swans at Coole – W.B. Yeats

The trees are in their autumn beauty;
The woodland paths are dry,
Under the October twilight the water
Mirrors a still sky;
Upon the brimming water among the stones
Are nine-and-fifty swans.

The nineteenth autumn has come upon me
Since first I made my count;
I saw, before I had well finished,
All suddenly mount

And scatter wheeling in great broken rings
Upon their clamorous wings.

I have looked upon those brilliant creatures,
And now my heart is sore.
All's changed since I, hearing at twilight,
The first time on this shore,
The bell-beat of their wings above my head,
Trod with a lighter tread.

Unwearied still, lover by lover,
They paddle in the cold
Companionable streams, or climb the air,
Their hearts have not grown old;
Passion or conquest, wander where they will,
Attend upon them still.

But now they drift on the still water,
Mysterious, beautiful:
Among what rushes will they build,
By what lake's edge or pool
Delight men's eyes when I awake some day
To find they have flown away?

## February 5th

The last poem has set my mind upon beauty, and what makes a poem purely beautiful – often it's simply a lyric poem with no especial depth of meaning that just catches your heart. The Elizabethans were particularly good at producing those short, heart-stopping verses, many of them, of course, intended to be set to music.: *Go Lovely Rose, My True Love Hath my Heart and I Have His, Adieu, Farewell Earth's Bliss, The Silver Swan;* and many others, they're just gorgeous. Here's one, anonymous, and set to music by Thomas Campion.

## Rose-cheek'd Laura – Anonymous

    Rose-cheek'd Laura, come;
Sing thou smoothly with thy beauty's
Silent music, either other
    Sweetly gracing.

    Lovely forms do flow
From conceit divinely framed:
Heaven is music, and thy beauty's
    Birth is heav'nly.

    Those dull notes we sing
Discords need for helps to grace them;
Only beauty purely loving
    Knows no discord;

    But still moves delight,
Like clear springs renew'd by flowing
Ever perfect, ever in them-
    Selves eternal.

## February 6th

Still thinking about beauty, and like an earworm, I can't get this strange poem by Emily Dickinson out of my head. She's obviously remembering Keats' famous lines at the end of the *Ode on a Grecian*

*Urn,* but whereas Keats sees perfect beauty as an eternal truth that transcends time and space, Dickinson is more ambiguous and elusive. Here it is one of her favourite companions, Death, who has joined the pair together. The two set up a dialogue, but they have 'failed' and in the end, the silence of the grave overtakes them both. I remember it as a long poem, but when I see it, I'm surprised to see how short it is; such is Dickinson's power of compression. But I don't feel I understand it.

**I Died For Beauty – Emily Dickinson**
I died for beauty, but was scarce
Adjusted in the tomb
When one who died for truth was lain
In an adjoining room.

He questioned softly why I failed,
'For beauty' I replied.
'And I for truth – themself are one,
We brethren are,' he said.

And so, as kinsmen met a night,
We talked between the rooms,
Until the moss had reached our lips,
And covered up our names.

**February 7$^{th}$**
Today's storm is called Imogen, and all night Imogen has been battering us with gusts of icy wind, and hurling needles of rain against the windows, sending rivers pouring down the road, and

inundating already saturated fields. More floods, more landslides, more perpetual wet.

The first appearance of Imogen was in Shakespeare's *Cymbeline*. It appears as such in the First Folio, but because of a casual mention by Simon Foreman, some modern commentators would like us to think that the real name is Innogen, with connotations of innocence and harmlessness. To me, Innogen sounds a harsh metallic name, like fuel for a nuclear reactor, or heavy-duty surface cleaner, whereas Imogen is softer and warmer. Imogen, the sweet heroine of Cymbeline, is disguised as a young man, and believed to be dead. Her long-lost brothers, not knowing who she is, sing this beautiful poem for her, now a favourite at funerals. I love the sibilant shudder and strange connotations of 'chimney-sweepers', though apparently to English children of the sixteenth century it was merely another name for dandelion heads. There's a touching personal note in the text when one of the brothers, Guiderius, says to Polydore that they must sing a funeral song, even though *'now our voices/Have got the mannish crack,'* suggesting that the voices of the two young actors had broken at the same time, so rendering them less useful for public singing; but Shakespeare wanted them to sing all the same.

## Fear no more – William Shakespeare
Fear no more the heat o' th' sun
Nor the furious winter's rages
Thou thy worldly task hast done,
Home art gone and ta'en thy wages;
Golden lads and girls all must,
As chimney sweepers, come to dust.

Fear no more the frown o' th' great;
Thou are past the tyrant's stroke
Care no more to clothe and eat,
To thee the reed is as the oak.
The sceptre, learning, physic must
All follow this and come to dust.
Fear no more the lightning flash,
Nor th' all dreaded thunder-stone
Fear not slander, censure rash,
Thou hast finish'd joy and moan.
All lovers young, all lovers must
Consign to thee and come to dust.

No exorcisor harm thee!
Nor no witchcraft harm thee!
Ghost unlaid forbear thee!
Nothing ill come near thee!
Quiet consummation have,
And renowned be thy grave!

## February 10th

We're in London, and have been invited to a secret magic concert of baroque music in the chapel of the Tower of London, emptied of all its tourists. Outside the Tower, we look at the dazzling embankment; the evening sky is a shimmering electric blue, and a thin sliver of moon rides next to the extravagantly illuminated Shard. The normally undistinguished buildings of the Embankment are transformed into fragile cages of light – it's a view to enter your soul and be always remembered.

The Tower is silent and remote, as our footsteps clatter on stones. Heavy walls shut us off from the noise and flash of the city; we are flung back in time to a place of ghosts and prisoners. In the chapel, as gorgeous music rises around us – a mixture of sixteenth-century music and modern settings of sixteenth-century texts, sung with dazzling harmonies by a young choir – we remember the ghosts we are sitting among, Anne Boleyn, Thomas More, Thomas Cromwell, and all those people who'd managed to annoy the monster that was Henry VIII.

Thomas Wyatt, one of the more attractive figures of the early sixteenth century, found himself, for reasons we don't quite know, imprisoned in the Tower at the same time that Anne Boleyn and her group of supposed lovers were being lined up for their bloody ends. Unlike them, though, he lived to tell the tale. We don't quite know how he escaped either – he'd certainly had a flirtation with Anne Boleyn in the early days, which should have been enough to ensure his death. His famous poem *Whoso List to Hunt* suggests that he has had to give way to the king in his passion; *There is written her fair neck around/Noli me tangere for Caesar's I am…* His biographer Nicola Schulman suggests that he might have given evidence against the young men – unpleasant if true.

But later he wrote a poem about those grim days. The Bell Tower is probably where he was imprisoned, and observed from his window the young men going to their deaths. The echoing refrain – *Circa Regna tonat* ('it thunders around thrones') describes the permanent unease of being to close to a king, especially one as unstable and vindictive as Henry.

## Who List His Wealth – Sir Thomas Wyatt

Who list his wealth and ease retain,
Himself let him unknown contain.
Press not too fast in at that gate
Where the return stands by disdain,
For sure, *circa Regna tonat*.

The high mountains are blasted oft
When the low valley is mild and soft.
Fortune with Health stands at debate.
The fall is grievous from aloft.
And sure, *circa Regna tonat*.

These bloody days have broken my heart.
My lust, my youth, did them depart,
And blind desire of estate.
Who hastes to climb seeks to revert.
Of truth, *circa Regna tonat*.

The bell tower showed me such sight
That in my head sticks day and night.
There did I learn out of a grate,
For all favour, glory, or might,
That yet *circa Regna tonat*.

By proof, I say, there did I learn:
Wit helpeth not defence too yerne,
Of innocency to plead or prate.
Bear low, therefore, give God the stern,
For sure, *circa Regna tonat*.

## February 14th

Here for Valentine's Day, another beautiful poem by Yeats, freely adapted from one by Pierre Ronsard. I like it, because it celebrates the tranquillity and calm that can come with old age – contrasted with Shakespeare's sonnets to his young man, in which he is obsessed by the effects of age on the young man's beauty and how it will diminish his assets; *when forty winters shall besiege thy brow.* Although in this poem, love 'has fled' the woman still retains her dignity and worth.

**When You Are Old – William Butler Yeats**
When you are old and gray and full of sleep
And nodding by the fire, take down this book,
And slowly read, and dream of the soft look
Your eyes once had, and of their shadows deep;

How many loved your moments of glad grace,
And loved your beauty with love false or true,
But one man loved the pilgrim soul in you,
And loved the sorrows of your changing face;

And bending down beside the glowing bars,
Murmur, a little sadly, how Love fled
And paced upon the mountain overhead
And hid his face amid a crowd of stars.

## February 16$^{th}$

Richard and I are both separately feeling angry with different people for various things – so a green scum of resentment and fury is creeping over the house in a nasty miasma, curling around corridors, rising up skirting boards, and licking its way upstairs and round the bannisters. Can a poem set it right? Well, if not quite, at least it can set a layer of something beautiful over the unpleasantness. Richard has found some lovely musical settings by Gerald Finzi of poems by Traherne. Of the three poets we associate with the Welsh border, Vaughan, Herbert and Traherne, Traherne seems to have been the nicest. We learn from their biographers that Vaughan could be unpleasant, and that Herbert was more ambitious and scratchy than he appears from his poems. But I've heard nothing against Traherne. And unusually for a sixteenth-century religious poet, he sees the joy, rather than the shame and sin, in his religion.

**Fullness – Thomas Traherne**

  That light, that sight, that thought,
 Which in my soul at first He wrought,
Is sure the only act to which I may
   Assent today;
  The mirror of an endless life
  The shadow of a virgin wife,
A spiritual world standing within,
  An Universe enclosed in skin,
My power exerted, or my perfect Being
If not enjoying, yet an act of seeing.
   My bliss
  Consists in this,
  My duty too
  In this I view.
  It is a fountain or a spring,
  Refreshing me in everything.
From whence those living streams I do derive,
By which my thirsty soul is kept alive.
  The centre and the sphere
  Of my delights are here. I felt a vigour in my sense.

## February 17th

Well, the tide of resentment hasn't quite ebbed, so I need a poem to mop it up. And this sonnet by Shakespeare belies its first line – it doesn't seem to be 'sweet silent thought' that he's enjoying here, but those middle-of-the-night sessions where grievances rise up out of nowhere and assume huge proportions. It's reassuring to think that Shakespeare could be as petty as the rest of us, going over and over grudges, *which I new if pay/as if not paid before,* lying awake perhaps in his attic lodging in Shoreditch, a dirty London moon glimmering in the window, a dead candle and an empty tankard on his table, along with the pile of papers he'd been working on that evening before the candle went out. Of course the poem ends with the rather glib conclusion that thinking of his lovely boy is enough to wipe out all these sorrows and losses, but in real life it doesn't quite work out that way, and I expect the poet went on with his grumbling thoughts until he fell asleep.

## Sonnet 30 – William Shakespeare

When to the sessions of sweet silent thought
I summon up remembrance of things past,
I sigh the lack of many a thing I sought,
And with old woes new wail my dear time's waste:
Then can I drown an eye, unused to flow,
For precious friends hid in death's dateless night,
And weep afresh love's long since cancelled woe,
And moan the expense of many a vanished sight:
Then can I grieve at grievances foregone,
And heavily from woe to woe tell o'er
The sad account of fore-bemoanèd moan,
Which I new pay as if not paid before.
But if the while I think on thee, dear friend,
All losses are restored and sorrows end.

## February 18th

A beautiful cold day today, a pale but brilliant sun, sending shimmering light over frosted grass and silvered branches, making deep shadows in the hills. Birds gather hungrily in the trees, little scraps of colour against the white. No cars have been past for as long as I've been standing here. Today's poem, posted on Facebook by a friend, just fits the mood of this pale, bright day. It's a day on which, at any rate here in the hills, nature seems stronger than anything mankind has added to the scene.

Sara Teasdale was an American poet of the late nineteeth century. Sickly and sensitive, she had much in common with Christina Rossetti, whom she admired and whose biography she wanted at one time to write. She was unhappily married, and had a long affair with the poet Vachel Lindsay. Both she and Lindsay died by suicide. Ray Bradbury wrote a well-known science fiction story titled after this poem.

### There will come soft rains – Sara Teasdale

There will come soft rains and the smell of the ground,
And swallows circling with their shimmering sound;
And frogs in the pools, singing at night,
And wild plum trees in tremulous white,
Robins will wear their feathery fire,
Whistling their whims on a low fence-wire;
And not one will know of the war, not one
Will care at last when it is done.
Not one would mind, neither bird nor tree,
If mankind perished utterly;
And Spring herself, when she woke at dawn,
Would scarcely know that we were gone.

**February 19th**

Thinking of Sara Teasdale, who's probably better known in America than here, made me remember another American woman poet of whom I knew absolutely nothing, Amy Lowell. Lowell (1874-1925) born into a smart Boston Brahmin family, was a cigar-smoking lesbian, and posthumously won the Pulitzer Prize for poetry. She belonged to the Imagist movement of the turn of the last century and introduced Imagist ideas to America. I find much of her poetry rather shapeless in a Whitmanesque sort of way, and she's prone to purple passages. But I like this; a poem about a certain sort of elevated and sensitive mood, maybe that which Keats calls 'negative capability' in which an ordinary and familiar scene takes on resonances and evocations beyond its commonplace appearance.

**Meeting House Hill – Amy Lowell**
I must be mad, or very tired,
When the curve of a blue bay beyond a railroad track
Is shrill and sweet to me like the sudden springing of a tune,
And the sight of a white church above thin trees in a city square
Amazes my eyes as though it were the Parthenon.
Clear, reticent, superbly final,
With the pillars of its porticoes refined to a cautious elegance,
It dominates the weak trees,
And the shot of its spire
Is cool, and candid,
Rising into an unresisting sky.
Strange meeting house
Pausing a moment upon a squalid hill-top.
I watch the spire sweeping the sky,
I am dizzy with movement of the sky;

I might be watching a mast
With its royals set full
Straining before a two-reef breeze.
I might be sighting a tea-clipper,
Tacking into the blue bay,
Just back from Canton
With her hold full of green and blue porcelain,
And a Chinese coolie leaning over the rail
Gazing at the white spire
With dull, sea-spent eyes.

## February 21st

Outside, it's a grey depressing day; too wet to go for a walk, everything misty in the gloom, sodden sheep chomping away on swedes like a dreary painting by Millet, everything still and hunched. I am without inspiration – no ideas for a poem of any sort. It should be a cue to try and write one, but alas, it doesn't work that way; writing obeys its own rules, and cheering you up in the gloom isn't among them. So taking the lazy way out, I simply google 'Grey day poem' and this pops up – another American poet whom I've never heard of, but it sort of suits today; a digression on how the human race survives through a myriad of dreary and humdrum tasks, and yet with a note of something like hope at the end that suggests that not only does it succeed in doing so, but is somehow inspired by the labour. William Vaughn Moody (1869-1910) was a university teacher, and in his day a fairly successful poet and dramatist. He seems to have been an austere, remote sort of man… a little grey, in fact.

## A Grey Day – William Vaughn Moody

Grey drizzling mists the moorlands drape,
Rain whitens the dead sea,
From headland dim to sullen cape
Grey sails creep wearily.
I know not how that merchantman
Has found the heart; but 'tis her plan
Seaward her endless course to shape.

Unreal as insects that appall
A drunkard's peevish brain,
O'er the grey deep the dories crawl,
Four-legged, with rowers twain;
Midgets and minims of the earth,
Across old ocean's vasty girth
Toiling – heroic, comical!

I wonder how the merchant's crew
Have ever found the will!
I wonder what the fishers do
To keep them toiling still!
I wonder how the heart of man
Has patience to live out its span
Or wait until its dreams come true.

## February 22nd

Probably the most translated poem ever must be the dying Emperor Hadrian's plaintive little address to his soul; it's been done hundreds of times by dozens of poets. I post a handful of them, including my own as the final one. It's a great loss to the English language that we've lost that diminutive affectionate noun ending, the equivalent of Hadrian's *-ula* ; *-kin* it would be, probably, or *-ette*, but all subsitutes are clumsy. Christina Rossetti, who didn't publish her version, seems to have unconsciously echoed Johnson's final words, but hers is an attractive poem nonetheless.

**Hadrian**
Animula vagula blandula,
Hospes comesque corporis,
Quae nunc abibis in loca
Pallidula rigida nudula,
Nec ut soles dabis jocos?

**Henry Vaughan**
My soul, my pleasant soul and witty,
The ghest and consort of my body,
Into what place now all alone,
Naked and sad wilt thou be gone,
No mirth, no wit as heretofore,
No jests wilt thou afford me more.

**Alexander Pope**
Ah! Fleeting Spirit! Wand'ring Fire
That long has warmed my tender Breast,
Must thou no more this frame inspire,
No more a pleasing cheerful guest?
Whither, ah whither art thou flying!
To what dark undiscover'd shore?
Thou see'st all trembling, shivering, dying,
And Wit and Humour are no more.

**Lord Byron**
Ah, gentle, fleeting wavering sprite,
Friend and associate of this clay!
To what unknown region borne
Wilt thou, now, wing thy distant flight?
No more with wonted humour gay
But pallid, cheerless and forlorn.

**Dr Johnson**
Oh loving soul, my own so tenderly,
My life's companion and my body's guest,
To what new realms, poor flutterer, wilt thou fly?
Cheerless disrobed, and cold in thy lone quest.
Hushed thy sweet fancies, mute thy wonted jest.

**Christina Rossetti**
Soul rudderless, unbraced,
The Body's friend and guest,
Whither away today?
Unsuppled, pale, discased,
Dumb to thy wonted jest.

**Frances**
Little soul, gentle soul,
Your lease here is done,
Where will you fly to
Cold and alone?
Naked and helpless
All laughter gone.

## February 23rd

Alice Meynell's poetry, faint, sweet and very Catholic, isn't normally to my taste, but I like this one, remembering the glorious electric-blue night sky over the Tower the other night. While her London skyline would have been very different from mine, she also loved what street lighting did to the evening skies over the city; the effect, as Richard reminded me, as Atkinson Grimshaw captures in his radiant and shimmering paintings of urban evenings. November is a long way away, but I'll post this anyway.

### November Blue – Alice Meynell

O heavenly colour, London town
    Has blurred it from her skies
And, hooded in an earthly brown,
    Unheaven'd the city lies.
No longer, standard-like, this hue
    Above the broad road flies;
Nor does the narrow street the blue
    Wear, slender pennon-wise.

But when the gold and silver lamps
    Colour the London dew,
And misted by the winter damps,
    The shops shine bright anew –
Blue comes to earth, it walks the street,
    It dyes the wide air through:
A mimic sky about their feet,
    The throng go crowned with blue.

## February 24th

A dazzling cold-burning sun is just melting the last of this morning's heavy frost, and spreading light on the hills. Yesterday, there was just a touch of spring warmth in the air, offering hope that the worst of the winter might be over (even though we've still got March to come, which can play nasty tricks on us.) Still, it gives us something to look forward to. Here's Tennyson, taking a break from the total misery of *In Memoriam,* also noting the arrival of Spring.

## In Memoriam CXIV – Alfred Lord Tennyson

Now fades the last long streak of snow,
    Now burgeons every maze of quick
    About the flowering squares, and thick
By ashen roots the violets blow.

Now rings the woodland loud and long,
    The distance takes a lovlier hue,
    And drown'd in yonder living blue
The lark becomes a sightless song.

Now dance the lights on lawn and lea,
    The flocks are whiter down the vale,
    And milkier every milky sail
On winding stream or distant sea:
Where now the seamew pipes, or dives
    In yonder greening gleam, and fly
    The happy birds, that change their sky
To build and brood; that live their lives

From land to land; and in my breast
    Spring wakens too; and my regret
    Becomes an April violet,
And buds and blossoms like the rest.

## February 26<sup>th</sup>

I first came across this poem when I was sitting in a London Underground train. Alas, there don't seem to be poems in the Underground any more – such a pity; it was lovely to sit there reading a poem, either a familiar one, or like this, one you'd never seen before. Although tiny, as short as a poem could be, it packs a punch; maybe it's the dramatic impact of that word 'hurl'd'; but the mind at once conjures up an image of all those bodies lying there, under Tudor rooftops, each unconscious, but each experiencing the startling adventure of their dreams.

    Sadly, I'm less of a dreamer than I used to be. I used to dream, vividly and dramatically, every night. I'd remember my dreams in the morning, and I felt sorry for those people who never remembered theirs – they were missing out on so much. But over the last few years, I've had to join their numbers – I don't always remember my dreams now, and when I do, they are mostly confused and muddled. Something has changed in my brain, I guess, but it does diminish my life. I used to find that dreams provided a guide to what was going on in my daytime thoughts; anxieties that sometimes you weren't even aware of surfaced in dreams; at other times, you experienced a guided tour to somewhere exotic and beautiful. I can vaguely remember bits of last night's dream – it was one of those standard anxiety-dreams, preparing for a holiday to some unspecified place. Of course, I was running late, had given myself barely an hour to pack, and in the end, I didn't seem to have my suitcase, only a make-up bag. When the taxi finally came, it turned out to be a hearse...

## Dreams – Robert Herrick
Here we all are, by day; at night we're hurl'd
By dreams, each one into a several world.

## February 27<sup>th</sup>

It's George Herbert Day today, apparently. Not that I need an excuse to post a George Herbert poem. As always in his poems, it's his personal, direct sense of God, the immediacy of his communication with Him, and the link of Heaven with the familiar everyday world, that jumps out at the reader.

## Redemption – George Herbert
Having been tenant long to a rich Lord,
    Not thriving, I resolved to be bold,
    And make suit unto him, to afford,
A new small-rented lease, and cancell th'old.
In heaven at his manour, I him sought;
    They told me there, that he was lately gone
    About some land, which he had dearly bought
Long since on earth, to take possession.
I straight return'd, and knowing his great birth,
    Sought him accordingly in great resorts:
    In cities, theatres, gardens, parks and courts;
At length I heard a ragged noise and mirth
    Of thieves and murderers: there him I espied,
Who straight, *Your suit is granted,* said, & died.

## February 28th

I've been looking through the manuscript of my original *Bracelet of Bright Hair*. It was much much longer than the version I published – mostly because I got rid of all poems in copyright, as I didn't want to get tangled up in copyright issues. But I found that I'd also cut out lots of poems for reasons I can't now remember. It was partly, I think, that losing modern poems had left my selection over-weighted with the nineteenth century – nothing wrong with that, but the nineteenth-century mood can become monotonous. But I think I probably hacked away at too much. Why on earth did I get rid of this, Shelley on the death of Keats – quite beautiful?

### *From* Adonais – Percy Bysshe Shelley

Peace, peace! he is not dead, he doth not sleep–
He hath awakened from the dream of life–
'Tis we, who lost in stormy visions, keep
With phantoms an unprofitable strife,
And in mad trance, strike with our spirit's knife
Invulnerable nothings.–We decay
Like corpses in a charnel; fear and grief
Convulse us and consume us day by day,
And cold hopes swarm like worms within our living clay.

He has outsoared the shadow of our night;
Envy and calumny and hate and pain,
And that unrest which men miscall delight,
Can touch him not and torture not again;
From the contagion of the world's slow stain

He is made one with Nature: there is heard
His voice in all her music, from the moan
Of thunder, to the song of night's sweet bird;

He is a presence to be felt and known
In darkness and in light, from herb and stone,
Spreading itself where'er that Power may move
Which has withdrawn his being to its own;
Which wields the world with never-wearied love,
Sustains it from beneath, and kindles it above.

He is a portion of the loveliness
Which once he made more lovely: he doth bear
His part, while the one Spirit's plastic stress
Sweeps through the dull dense world, compelling there
Torturing th' unwilling dross that checks its flight
To its own likeness, as each mass may bear;
And bursting in its beauty and its might
From trees and beasts and men into the Heaven's light.

## February 29<sup>th</sup>

Here's another poem I left out, quite inexplicably, especially as my younger daughter's second name is Alyson – a beautiful medieval love poem.

*Between March and April*
*When spray begins to spring,*
*The little bird has her will*
*Of her lord to sing.*
*I live in love-longing*
*For the best, the sweetest thing*
*She shall me rapture bring,*
*I am quite in her thrall:*
*A lovely chance has come my way,*
*From Heaven it's come, I hope and pray,*

> *From others my love has flown away,*
> *And lights on Alysoun.*

It doesn't really matter if you can't read Middle English – most of it makes its own sense.

>Lossum – lovesome
>Wonges – cheeks ('my cheeks grow pale')
>Make – mate
>Tholien – to suffer
>Reve – take away (like 'reiver')

## Alysoun – Anon

Between Merch and Averil,
When spray beginneth to springe,
The litel fowl hath hire wil
On hire leod to singe.
Ich libbe in love-longinge
For semlokest of alle thinge.
Heo may me blisse bringe:
Ich am in hire baundoun.
*An hendy hap ich habbe yhent,*
*Ichot from Heaven it is me sent,*
*From alle women my love is lent,*
*And light on Alysoun.*
On heu hire her is fayr ynoh
Hire browe broune, her eye blake;
With lossum chere he on me loh;
With middel small and well ymake.
But heo me wolle to hire take
For to been hire owen make,
Longe to liven ichulle forsake,

And feye fallen adoun,
*An hendy hap etc*
Nightes when I wend and wake,
Forthy mine wonges waxeth wan:
Levedy, al for thine sake
Longinge is ylent me on.
In world is noon so witer man
That al hire bountee telle can:
Hire swire is whittere than the swan,
And fairest may in town.
*An hendy hap etc*
Icham for wowing al forwake,
Wery so water in wore.
Lest any reve me my make
Ich habbe y-yerned yore.
Bettere is tholien whuile sore
Than mournen evermore.
Geinest under gore,
Herkne to my roun:
*An hendy hap …*

# *March*

## March 1<sup>st</sup>

There has to be a Welsh poem for St David's Day, and I was moved by this, from the nineteenth-century Welsh poet, John Lloyd. The red kite has been one of the great British conservation success stories of recent times; when we first came to Wales, their numbers had dwindled to a few breeding pairs near Abergwesyn. There'd been attempts to conserve them through the twentieth century, starting with a vicar in the Twenties who'd paid farmers to protect nests from gamekeepers and egg-collectors, but despite his efforts and those of lots of nice people on bicycles, the numbers hadn't increased. Red kites are untidy nest builders and lay very few eggs, so they aren't naturally prolific. But it was a farmer's wife near Aberystwyth, who defying all the rules of conservation, fed them with butcher's meat and the numbers began to grow. Now there are several red kite feeding centres in Wales, and the birds are a common sight. We had one over our house the other day – it's lovely to watch their swooping wheeling flight, and to catch the brilliant scarlet of their feathers in sunlight. Now we see more kites than buzzards, and we almost take them for granted. Incidentally, the native British red kites are shy birds who tend to stay in Wales – the ones you see in large numbers over the Oxford motorway are Spanish intruders, brought in some years ago to boost the population. (*They come over here, take our carrion…*)

And of the other creatures Lloyd mentions, it's not all doom and gloom. We see plenty of magpies, so many that I run out of poem to count them, hear owls nearly every night, and always have a black and white woodpecker or two in the garden. The squirrels, presumably the red ones, have all gone, alas, except in Anglesey, superseded by those clever crooks, the greys, against whom Richard wages a continual but futile war. And I imagine that Lloyd would have seen more wild flowers and butterflies than we do today. And we don't have the variety of birds at our bird table any more – we used to have goldcrests, wagtails, tree creepers and yellowhammers – now we just seem to be deluged with blue tits and chaffinches. But it's interested to see someone in the nineteenth century so interested in conservation issues.

## *From* Thoughts of Boyhood – John Lloyd

Well I remember in my boyish hours
    Gazing with rapture on the fantailed kite
As hovering full o'er Brecknock's ivied towers
    Slowly he wheeled his solitary flight.

Now low, as though within the mirror clear
    Of Usk's fair bosom he his form admired
Now like the tenant of some loftier sphere,
    A speck amid the far-off clouds retired.

And often in our blithest, noisiest mood,
    When yet unseen his shrill cry told him near,
Up-gazing that mysterious form we viewed
    With a long look of wonderment and fear.

Now 'mid the landscape is he seen no more
    Fanning his broad wings in the noontide sun,
Scared from his circuit on that 'customed shore
    By prowling keeper armed with trap and gun.

In lone Cwmserri where the thunder clouds,
    For so its name implies, delight to rest,
In the dark bosom of the Vunglas woods,
    Alike the spoilers robbed him of his nest.

Nor his alone they seek: the bustling jay
    And playful squirrel too they vermin call;
Each harmless, helpless thing alike they slay
    To make a show along their kennel wall.

Hence with each year more dull our woods become,
    The tapping woodpecker, the chattering pie,
Now rarely heard: the whooping owl is dumb,
    The raven calls not to his mate on high.

## March 3$^{rd}$

A poem about a dark, despairing world, but one that has a glimmer of hope at its conclusion. Laurence Binyon, an art historian and poet, was too old to fight in the First World War, but he worked as a medical orderly, and wrote the famous 'For the Fallen' (*They shall not grow old/ as we that are left grow old.*) He was also an eminent art historian, who specialised in oriental art and worked for many years as Keeper of Prints and Drawings at the British Museum.

### The Winds Of All The World – Laurence Binyon

The winds of all the world bring agonies,
Day by day, hour by hour, into our ears;
Not only desolation, blood, and tears,
But cloud on cloud of suffocating lies.

The human strives with the inhuman there,
Enduring things beyond belief, and still
Because of one unconquerable will
Confronts, clear-eyed, what it has yet to bear.

Before the sunrise, under naked trees
On grass that sparkled in the dew, I paced.
I thought of all the torment, all the waste;
I thought of beauty, justice, mercy, peace.

Beyond the raging of the powers of night
What from of old stood, still was dear, was true.
Far in the East the sky to glory grew,
And slowly earth rolled onward into light.

## March 5<sup>th</sup>

I was reminded the other day of Christopher Marlowe, when we watched *As You Like It* streamed to our local cinema from the National Theatre, and heard Shakespeare cheekily but affectionately quoting Marlowe, then recently murdered, *Dead shepherd,* Phoebe says, *now I find thy saw of might/Whoever loved that loved not at first sight* And not long after, Touchstone complains that *When a man's verses are not understood…it strikes a man more dead than a great reckoning in a little room*, a reference to the famous 'reckoning' or bill, in Southwark which is supposed to have started the quarrel that led to Marlowe's death. Marlowe is one of the most enigmatic figures in Elizabethan poetry. Just two months older than Shakespeare, the son of a shoemaker from Canterbury, he was killed in 1593, at the height of his powers. Mysteries abound. Was he a spy? Was he a heretic? Was he gay? Was his death a state execution? At any rate, he wrote some of the most stunning verse in English. Not all his work is consistently good – I remember seeing *Tamburlaine* years ago, and not really enjoying it. But the best is wonderful; including extraordinary one-liners: *Is this the face that launched a thousand ships? / Why, this is hell, nor am I out of it. / Infinite riches in a little room* (hence Shakespeare's quote in *As You Like It* – I bet he was jealous of that line.) It's a pity that the ascendancy of Shakespeare has meant that less attention is paid to some of the marvellous poets who were his contemporaries. *Doctor Faustus* is full of magnificent poetry, though Faustus doesn't have the psychological depth of Shakespeare's characters. But Faustus, though he's guilty of pride, isn't an unsympathetic figure. He's greedy for knowledge, and the power that knowledge will give; (as a child I found it bewildering that Adam and Eve were expelled from Paradise for seeking knowledge.) We share some of Faustus's excitement, though he knows from the start that he's doomed to Hell. Yet in the moment when he understands that his fate is close, he feels the implications as if for the first time. It's impossible to read his speech, the last in the play, without catching your breath.

## *From* Doctor Faustus – Christopher Marlowe

Ah Faustus,
Now hast thou but one bare hour to live,
And then thou must be damn'd perpetually!
Stand still, you ever-moving spheres of heaven,
That time may cease and midnight never come:
Fair Nature's eye, rise, rise again and make
Perpetual day; or let this hour be but
A year, a month, a week, a natural day
That Faustus may repent and save his soul!
*O lente, lente currite, noctis equi!*
The stars move still, time runs, the clock will strike,

The devil will come, and Faustus must be damned,
O, I'll leap up to my God! –Who pulls me down?–
See, see, where Christ's blood streams in the firmament!
One drop would save my soul, half a drop, ah my Christ!–
Ah rend not my heart for naming of my Christ!
Yet will I call on him; O spare me, Lucifer......

..........Ah! half the hour is past! 'Twill all be past anon.
O God,
If thou wilt not have mercy on my soul,
Yet for Christ's sake, whose blood hath ransom'd me,
Impose some end to my incessant pain:
Let Faustus live in hell a thousand years,
A hundred thousand, and at last be sav'd!
O, no end is limited to damned souls!

Why wert thou not a creature wanting soul?

Or why is this immortal that thou hast?........
........                    *(the clock strikes twelve)*
O it strikes, it strikes! Now body turn to air,
Or Lucifer will bear thee quick to hell!
                    *(thunder and lightning)*
O soul, be chang'd into little water-drops,
And fall into the ocean, ne'er be found!
                    *(Enter Devils)*

My God, my God, look not so fierce on me!
Adders and serpents, let me breathe a while!
Ugly hell, gape not, come not, Lucifer!
I'll burn my books – Ah, Mephistophilis!
                    *(Exeunt Devils with Fautus)*

# March 8<sup>th</sup>

Two nice anniversaries to celebrate today – my elder daughter's birthday, and International Women's Day. The world in which my daughter grew up is a better one for her in many ways than it would have been some generations ago – she has a wide selection of life choices, and is able to regard herself as a human being rather than just an adjunct to, or possession of, a man. Yet in many countries in the world, women are still treated with cruelty and contempt; and even in our society, internet trolling shows the truly poisonous attitude towards women that still exists.

It's hard to find poems about women – modern ones tend to be rather drearily inspirational, and older ones take an Angel in the House line, but Elizabeth Barratt Browning, though her poetry isn't much read today, wrote with a strong and perceptive intelligence, and had a vivid understanding of the role women had to play in nineteenth century society. Here's Aurora Leigh writing about her education at the hands of her narrow-minded aunt.

## *From* Aurora Leigh – Elizabeth Barratt Browning

Because she liked accomplishments in girls
I read a score of books on womanhood,
To prove, if women do not think at all,
They may teach thinking (to a maiden-aunt
Or else the author,) – books that boldly assert
Their right of comprehending husband's talk
When not too deep, and even of answering
With pretty 'may it please you' or 'so it is' –
Their rapid insight and fine aptitude,
Particular worth and general missionariness,
As long as they keep quiet by the fire,
And never say 'no' when the world says 'aye,'

For that is fatal – their angelic reach
Of virtue, chiefly used to sit and darn,
And fatten household sinners – their, in brief
Potential facility in everything
Of abdicating power in it; she owned
She liked a woman to be womanly,
And English women, she thanked God and sighed
(Some people always sigh in thanking God)
Were models to the universe…

## March 9th

A grey day today, driving rain, surging wind and a sky like dirty cotton wool. All the colours of the world leached out; no brightness in the greens and browns around us. Trees in a gloomy leafless huddle. And the usual assortment of horrible world news. So I want a brave, bold, colourful poem today. Quite hard to find one, but then I turn to Gerard Manley Hopkins. Hopkins, though he had his times of despair and depression, was always alive to the beauty and splendour of the world – something I didn't find in the Catholicism in which I was brought up.

But here's Hopkins with beauty and spring in one poem – sin is present, of course, his Catholic sensibility doesn't dare to leave it out, but it's secondary here to the sensory glories he describes. It's one of his best known poems, but it can always bear being looked at again, especially since many people won't have re-read it since schooldays. I love the imagery of the 'glassy peartree' – the bright sunlight of spring making the blossom-laden tree seem transparent. And the weeds growing out of wheels. Especially I love the blues in this poem – the thrushes' eggs, and the blue of the sky 'all in a rush' – it reminds me of the evening blues of Alice Meynell's poem. Of course to Catholic Hopkins and Meynell, blue would hold the same beloved connotation of the Virgin Mary. The edification of the Virgin must have been a welcome addition to the harsh theology of medieval Catholicism. Blue became identified as Mary's colour, because it's a beautiful colour that goes particularly well with gold, and you would show respect and veneration for her by having to invest in precious ultramarine. Incidentally, when I was a child, if you asked a girl what her favourite colour was, she would reply 'blue' (boys would say 'red'.) The preponderance of sickly pink as girls' favourite colour is something that's been commercially driven only in recent years.

Anyway, here's this poem with its beautiful blues.

## Spring – Gerard Manley Hopkins

Nothing is so beautiful as spring –
    When weeds, in wheels, shoot long and lovely and lush;
    Thrush's eggs look little low heavens, and thrush
Through the echoing timber does so rinse and wring
The ear, it strikes like lightnings to hear him sing;
    The glassy peartree leaves and blooms, they brush
    The descending blue; the blue is all in a rush
With richness; the racing lambs too have fair their fling.

What is all this juice and all this joy?
    A strain of the earth's sweet being in the beginning
In Eden garden – Have, get, before it cloy,
    Before it cloud, Christ, lord, and sour with sinning,
Innocent mind and Mayday in girl and boy,
    Most, O maid's child, thy choice and worthy the winning.

## March 10th

And here today, with our own sky a very clear, but pale blue, is another poem about the colour blue, though Lawrence takes an unexpected turn by identifying his blues not with heaven, but with Pluto's dark hell. Lawrence veers between being deeply annoying and startlingly good, the most contrary of writers; but the imagery of this poem burns into your brain, as he turns his intense and obsessive eye onto a world of darkness upon darkness, with the blue of the flowers becoming torches into an underground and deathly kingdom.

## Bavarian Gentians – D.H. Lawrence

Not every man has gentians in his house,
In Soft September, at slow, Sad Michaelmas.
Bavarian gentians, big and dark, only dark
Darkening the day-time, torch-like with the smoking blueness of Pluto's gloom,
Ribbed and torch-like, with their blaze of darkness spread blue
down flattening into points, flattened under the sweep of white day
torch-flower of the blue-smoking darkness, Pluto's dark-blue daze,
black lamps from the halls of Dis, burning dark blue,
giving off darkness, blue darkness, as Demeter's pale lamps give off light,
lead me then, lead me the way.

Reach me a gentian, give me a torch
let me guide myself with the blue, forked torch of this flower
down the darker and darker stairs, where blue is darkened on blueness,
even where Persephone goes, just now, from the frosted September

to the sightless realm where darkness is awake upon the dark
and Persephone herself is but a voice
or a darkness invisible enfolded in the deeper dark
of the arms Plutonic, and pierced with the passion of dense gloom,
among the splendour of torches of darkness, shedding darkness
on the lost bride and her groom.

## March 11th

My last poetry diary was called *A Bracelet of Bright Hair*, chosen because the words are lovely, but also because it suggested to me a collection of lovely things. The title for this collection comes from Milton's *L'Allegro;*

> *And the jocund rebecks sound*
> *To many a youth and many a maid*
> *Dancing in the Chequer'd shade.*

The world and our lives are darker now than they were when I wrote that last diary, though many things in it are still bright for me, and this hints of that contrast.

We saw Milton's *L'Allegro*, set to music by Handel, and performed by the inimitable Mark Morris dancers at the ENO many years ago; one of the most exciting theatrical events I've witnessed. Though Milton's voice in *L'Allegro* doesn't seem quite comfortable for him – he can do grandeur, despair, melancholy, even sensuality, but simple jollity isn't quite his thing. So today's poem comes from Blake's *Auguries of Innocence* – as many of the poems I choose, it's something that's been running through my head for days.

***From* Auguries of Innocence – William Blake**
Man was made for joy and woe;
And when this we rightly know,
Thro' the world we safely go.
Joy and woe are woven fine,
A clothing for the soul divine;
Under every grief and pine
Runs a joy with silken twine…

## March 12th

Spending a day or so on the Cardigan coast at a favourite hotel. We set off intending to find a bit of cliff to walk along, but instead are diverted to a National Trust house and garden. The house is closed, but the garden and farm are open, and we wander among piggeries and stables, walled gardens and Victorian plantings of rhododendrons and wellingtonia. We find a lake full of bulrushes, and caught in a benediction of sunshine, sit down on a bench. I've never been a sun person – a holiday where sun was the main attraction would be my idea, in the words of the song, of nothing to do. Autumn and spring are my preferred seasons; I like to see winter trees with their tangle of bare branches; I like the quiet and shyer flowers of spring. Many people talk of their childhoods as being a succession of summer days, but my memories seem to be of cold winter afternoons; rather than splashing through sunlit waves, I remember sitting on one of our big armchairs, by a coal fire and reading a book which transported me to wonderful new worlds (I was an only child as you can possibly tell.) But this winter, for the first time, I've been oppressed by the greyness and the wetness of it, the endless battering of rain, the soggy grass, the flooded fields, the chill seeping through the air, the cloudy sodden skies. And not being quite as well as I'd like to be makes me feel as though I'm made of tissue paper, and the cold seeps through me and crumples me up. But today, almost for the first time, I'm loving the sun falling on me like honey; I can feel it warming me through and turning the tissue paper back to flesh.

The best sun celebration is the Beatles song but it can't go here. I can't quite find a poem that says all I want to say, so I've had to write it myself.

**The Day The Sun Came Out**
The day the sun came out, people said
We must build our house upon the hill
We must plant our beans with the scarlet flowers,
Paint a new colour on the door,
Take out our silver dancing shoes,
Pack our winter coats away in trunks,
Fly our kites upon the heath,
Spread out our maps upon the table.

The day the sun came out,
The celandines were polished gold,
The blue sky tipped into the lake,
Birds put on their crimson jackets,
All the daisies opened their eyes,
The ladybird came out and tried her wings,
Catkins waggled their tails,
Hedges untangled their thorns,
Trees remembered their leaves.

All of these things happened
On the day the sun came out.

# March 17th

St Patrick's Day today, but though I had an Irish grandfather, I don't feel entitled to celebrate it. We've only been to Ireland once; I remember it as a magical place of huge silver beaches, ruined great houses and green hills. And friendly local people leaving fresh mackerel on our doorstep. Part of me doesn't want to go back because I know it will all be changed now – what I remember was partly the picturesqueness of poverty. I also remember the shops selling nothing but potatoes, cabbage and scrag end of lamb, and the children who looked poor in the way that London children didn't. We fetched up in New York on St Patrick's Day some years later; this was in the days when Americans enthusiastically supported the IRA; and as we watched a St Patrick's procession going noisily down Columbus Avenue, didn't dare to open our mouths just in case someone heard our English accents. But I remember from that day a rather beautiful, and obviously mad, young man, dressed like Jesus, and solemnly blessing the procession as it passed.

An Irish poem? Well, this is a good excuse for Panguar Ban, written down on the pages of a manuscript by an Irish monk in the ninth century, here in the famous translation by Robin Flower. I love this poem, partly because of its charm, but also because it supplies a more gentle side to the otherwise grim picture of Celtic monasticism.

**Panguar Ban –** *Translation from the Irish by* **Robin Flower.**
I and Panguar Ban my cat
'Tis a like task we are at;
Hunting mice is his delight,
Hunting words I sit all night.

Better far than praise of men
'Tis to sit with book and pen;
Panguar bears me no ill-will,
He too plies his simple skill.

'Tis a merry task to see
At our tasks how glad are we,
When at home we sit and find
Entertainment to our mind.

Oftentimes a mouse will stray
In the hero Panguar's way;
Oftentimes my keen thought set
Takes a meaning in its net.

'Gainst the wall he sets his eye
Full and fierce and sharp and sly;
'Gainst the wall of knowledge I
All my little wisdom try.

When a mouse darts from its den,
O how glad is Panguar then!
O what gladness do I prove
When I solve the doubts I love!

So in peace our task we ply,
Panguar Ban, my cat and I;
In our arts we find our bliss,
I have mine and he has his.

Practice every day has made
Panguar perfect in his trade;
I get wisdom day and night
Turning darkness into light.

## March 20th

Palm Sunday and the first official day of spring today, so there ought to be a poem around somewhere. But lazily we don't go to church, and our spring walk about the local lake is cold and windy, so we're muffled up in hats and gloves. Still the lake is full of wildlife, swans and geese and mallards, and birds that Richard tells me are coots and terns; and if we're all huddled and cold, the birds certainly aren't. They're all excited, looking for nesting places in the bulrushes, fetching twigs, questing for mates. Swans flap lazily through the water, their great wings splashing, colourful male mallards chase females rather unpleasantly (their courtships aren't too nice.) Black-headed gulls are massing around the rim of the lake where people bring food. I see a very small duck trying to thump a very large swan; but the swan is in a genial mood and simply brushes him aside with a flick of feathers.

For spring, here is one of Christina Rossetti's calm and deceptively simple poems.

### Spring – Christina Rossetti
Gone were but the Winter,
Come were but the Spring,
I would go to a covert
Where the birds sing:

Where in the whitethorn
Singeth a thrush,
And a robin sings
In the holly-bush.

Full of fresh scents
Are the budding boughs
Arching high over
A cool green house:

Full of sweet scents,
And whispering air
Which sayeth softly:
'We spread no snare:

'Here dwell in safety,
Here dwell alone,
With a clear stream
And a mossy stone.

Here the sun shineth
Most shadily:
Here is heard an echo
Of the far sea,
Tho' far off it be.'

## March 21st

Life in the back-of-beyond where we live is surprisingly full of cultural activity – lots of singing for Richard, drawing classes for me, and for both of us, a Shakespeare reading group. It's organised by Philip Bowen and Sue Best, who run the Willow Globe Theatre near Rhyader, an open-air theatre made from living willow trees; a beautiful space in which to hear poetry. In the winter, it's a fragile cage of branches, but in spring, it suddenly bursts into hazy filigree of green, a magical space where you feel you will meet Titania tended by Cobweb, Peaseblossom, Moth and Mustard Seed, sleeping against a scented bank.

We meet to read a Shakespeare play every two weeks – but it's not like the bad old days of going round the class stumbling over the lines at school. Phil and Sue know more about Shakespeare, about poetry and stagecraft than you can imagine, and we come away with a deep insight and understanding of the text that just reading the lines through at home can never produce.

I asked Richard to suggest a poem for me to include in this diary, and he came up with Mercutio's Queen Mab speech from our current play, *Romeo and Juliet.*

Mercutio must be Shakespeare's most attractive character – apparently Shakespeare said that he had to kill him off, otherwise he would have taken over the whole play. This speech is a long riff on dreams and romantic melancholy – it starts off as a gentle and very funny parody on faery-pastoral, and becomes a brilliant swoop into the workings of the subconscious mind and the weirdness of dreams. He's mocking Romeo's impassioned and exaggerated love for Rosaline, appropriately, for in a very short time Romeo will be just as extravagantly in love with someone else. Love, Mercutio says, is just one of the sneaky tricks Queen Mab plays on hapless mortals. Here Shakespeare takes us deep into the stories of English folklore that he heard in his youth, the boggarts and elves and pucks, simple and mischievous spirits, so different from the elegant classical creatures from Ovid and the ancient poets that he also knew and loved. But you feel that these stories went deeper into his soul than the gods and goddesses, and made the English countryside resonate with magic for him, its deep secrets braided into the woods and fields all around him.

## Mercutio's speech *from* Romeo and Juliet – William Shakespeare

O then, I see Queen Mab hath been with you.
She is the fairies' midwife, and she comes
In shape no bigger than an agate-stone
On the fore-finger of an alderman,
Drawn with a team of little atomies
Athwart men's noses as they lie asleep;
Her wagon-spokes made of long spinners' legs,
The cover of the wings of grasshoppers,
The traces of the smallest spider's web,
The collars of the moonshine's watery beams,
Her whip of cricket's bone, the lash of film,
Her wagoner a small grey-coated gnat,
Not so big as a round little worm
Prick'd from the lazy finger of a maid;
Her chariot is an empty hazel-nut
Made by the joiner squirrel or old grub,
Time out o' mind the fairies' coachmakers.
And in this state she gallops night by night
Through lovers' brains, and then they dream of love…

## March 22nd

Apparently it's World Poetry Day today, whatever that means. But little to celebrate this morning, with news of a friend's serious illness, and of the atrocity in Belgium. Nothing really seems appropriate to these circumstances, but I think of an unjustly ignored poem by the much maligned Mrs Hemans, whom no-one can quite forgive for *Casabianca (The boy stood on the burning deck.)* Yet she was a serious poet, Welsh by adoption, who supported a large family by writing. This is a gloomy, but magnificent poem, I think.

## The Hour of Death – Felicia Hemans

Leaves have their time to fall.
And flowers to wither at the north wind's breath,
And stars to set – but all,
Thou hast *all* seasons for thine own, O Death!

Day is for mortal care,
Eve, for glad meetings round the joyous hearth,
Night, for the dreams of sleep, the voice of prayer –
But all for thee, thou mightiest of the earth.

The banquet hath its hour –
Its feverish hour, of mirth and song and wine;
There comes a day for grief's o'erwhelming power,
A time for softer tears – but all are thine.

Youth and the opening rose
May look like things too glorious to decay,
And smile at thee – but thou are not of those
That wait the ripened bloom to seize their prey.

Leaves have their time to fall,
And flowers to wither at the north wind's breath,
And stars to set – but all,
Thou hast *all* seasons for thine own, O Death!

We know when moons shall wane,
When summer birds from far shall cross the sea,
When autumn's hue shall tinge the golden grain –
But who shall teach us when to look for thee?

Is it when spring's first gale
Comes forth to whisper where the violets lie?
Is it when roses in our paths grow pale?–
They have one season – *all* are ours to die!

Thou art there where billows foam,
Thou art where music melts upon the air;
Thou art around us in our peaceful home,
And the world calls us forth – and thou art there.

Thou art where friend meets friend,
Beneath the shadow of the elm to rest –
Thou art where foe meets foe, and trumpets rend
The skies, and swords beat down the princely crest.

Leaves have their time to fall,
And flowers to wither at the north wind's breath,
And stars to set – but all–
Thou hast *all* seasons for thine own, O Death

## March 23rd

Spring can be a melancholy season, as well as an exciting one. Here's a sad little poem by that enigmatic poet of the late nineteenth and early twentieth century, Charlotte Mew. She was admired by many poets, including Hardy, Masefield and Sassoon. She took her own life at the age of forty-nine.

## I So Liked Spring – Charlotte Mew

I so liked Spring last year
Because you were here –
The thrushes too –
Because it was these you so liked to hear –
I so liked you.

This year's a different thing, –
I'll not think of you.
But I'll like Spring because it is simply Spring
As the thrushes do.

## March 24th

Maunday Thursday, and, as most days have been recently, a cold grey day, threatening rain, suitable weather for Passiontide, except that the forecasters are also promising the same grim weather for Easter. The Last Supper is one of those gospel narratives where the story comes vividly to life – the strange instruction of Christ to his disciples to look for a man carrying a pitcher of water, to follow him to his house, and demand to use the upper room for the Passover feast, the details of feet-washing, of towels, of breaking bread and drinking wine, and Jesus's ominous hints about betrayals. It's a narrative full of menace and the sense of horrors, but also great things to come.

This is a marvellous poem about that night, written by Rilke in 1906, after seeing Leonardo Da Vinci's ruined masterpiece of the scene. The poet suggests that the apostles feel that Jesus, about to embark alone on his strange and violent destiny, is no longer their familiar friend, their possession, but someone who belongs to the world.

## The Last Supper – Rainer Maria Rilke
## (tr Margarete Münsterberg)

Here they are gathered, wondering and deranged,

Round Him, who wisely doth Himself inclose,
And who now takes Himself away, estranged,
From those who owned him once, and past them flows.
He feels the ancient loneliness to-day
That taught Him all His deepest acts of love;
Now in the olive groves He soon will rove,
And these who love Him all will flee away.

To the last supper table He hath led,
As birds are frightened from a garden-bed
By shots, so He their hands forth from the bread
Doth frighten by His word: to Him they flee:
Then flutter round the table in their fright
And seek a passage from the hall. But He
Is everywhere, like dusk at fall of night.

## March 25<sup>th</sup> – Good Friday

By 1613, marriage and family cares had irrevocably changed the hedonistic young John Donne, who had written *For God's sake, hold your tongue and let me love*, into a troubled, anxious and impoverished figure. Holding her tongue and letting him love had already given poor Anne Donne several children – she was to give birth to twelve altogether, of whom seven would survive into adulthood, but the birth of the twelfth would kill her in 1616. Donne had been restless and uneasy for the last few years – he had not yet entered the church, but would do so shortly. He'd attached himself to wealthy patrons, and had spent the last few months travelling around Europe, while Anne at home had a miscarriage. In the spring, he was off again, this time to stay with Sir Edward Herbert, brother of George, and son of Donne's patroness, Magdalen, in Montgomery Castle. It's an odd poem, partly justifying, one feels, his absence to Anne, but also the fact that by riding westwards, he's turning his back on Jesus, who died in the East. Jesus's death, he suggests, is too much for him to contemplate; as a sinner, he'll need to be purified first. He's doubtful of God's mercy; something we hear even in his later religious poems (*Except you enthrall me, never shall be free, Nor ever chaste unless you ravish mee.*)

There's an extra treat for us this afternoon – Richard's choir is putting on a performance at a local church with readings from St Matthew's Passion and music by Bach, Purcell, Stainer etc. The highlights for me were two poetry readings, given by Philip Bowen of the Willow Globe Theatre, of R.S. Thomas's *The Coming* and John Donne's *Riding Westwards*, which coincidentally I'd already chosen as my poem for the day. Poetry reading can be a strange and difficult task – too often the reading adds nothing but a kind of poetic flummery to the words rather than illuminating them, but Philip's careful, measured and utterly intelligent rendition gave this difficult poem a shape and cohesion which I'd been finding hard to get from just reading it in my head.

## Good Friday 1613; Riding Westward – John Donne
Let man's soul be a sphere, and then, in this,
Th' intelligence that moves, devotion is;

And as the other spheres, by being grown
Subject to foreign motion, lose their own,
And being by others hurried every day,
Scarce in a year their natural form obey;
Pleasure or business, so, our souls admit
For their first mover, and are whirl'd by it.
Hence is't, that I am carried towards the west,
This day, when my soul's form bends to the East.
There I should see a Sun by rising set,
And by that setting endless day beget.
But that Christ on His cross did rise and fall,
Sin had eternally benighted all.
Yet dare I almost be glad, I do not see
That spectacle of too much weight for me.
Who sees Gods face, that is self-life, must die;
What a death were it then to see God die?
It made His own lieutenant, Nature, shrink,
It made His footstool crack, and the sun wink.
Could I behold those hands, which span the poles
And tune all spheres at once, pierced with those holes?
Could I behold that endless height, which is
Zenith to us and our antipodes,
Humbled below us? or that blood, which is
The seat of all our soul's, if not of His,
Made dirt of dust, or that flesh which was worn
By God for His apparel, ragg'd and torn?
If on these things I durst not look, durst I
On His distressed Mother cast mine eye,
Who was God's partner here, and furnish'd thus
Half of that sacrifice which ransom'd us?
Though these things as I ride be from mine eye,

They're present yet unto my memory,
For that looks towards them ; and Thou look'st towards me,
O Saviour, as Thou hang'st upon the tree.
I turn my back to thee but to receive
Corrections till Thy mercies bid Thee leave.
O think me worth Thine anger, punish me,
Burn off my rust, and my deformity;
Restore Thine image, so much, by Thy grace,
That Thou may'st know me, and I'll turn my face.

## March 26<sup>th</sup>

Richard loves feeding our garden birds, though they get through an inordinate amount of nuts and seeds; a friend of ours regards this as 'spoiling their characters.' Still, they're pretty to watch, and in the past we've had a variety of them, though nowadays they're usually chaffinches and blue tits. The downsides are the ever attentive sparowhawks, and the occasional casualty flying into our windows. I found a dead bullfinch this morning, and a dead chaffinch too, after I'd written this poem.

### Dead Bullfinch

You thought you flew at air,
Your soft and tender element,
But it was glass, hard glass,
And caught and killed you there.

Black feathers curled like fingers,
Your crimson breast all bare,
But all your colours radiant still. You were a rare

And nervous guest among us. Yet we care
For this small death amidst so many more this Easter
Smashed beyond repair.

## March 27<sup>th</sup> – Easter Day

We go off in the morning – horribly early, it seems – the clocks have just gone forward – to the Eucharist service in our lovely little twelfth-century church. A momentary lick of sunshine brightens everything up, and the interior glows with the displays of daffodils and evergreens that careful and loving hands have prepared for us. We sing our halleluias that Jesus Christ has risen again – and listen to the compelling narrative of the Resurrection from St John's Gospel – another magnificent piece of storytelling, with the disciples running to the tomb, one outstripping the other, the empty tomb and the napkin folded apart, and then Mary thinking she sees the gardener, until he speaks. As always, it's the details that give life to these stories.

But somehow I can't help my agnostic spirit grumbling meanly and I wonder why we all need to be redeemed for a sin none of us were around to commit. Meanwhile, Sin still rampages unchecked in the world, as the two atrocities we hear about today show us horribly – children and their mothers killed in a park, little boys killed returning from a football match. I guess if you have faith everything falls into place. I had faith once, so I can remember what it feels like; but it's gradually dissipated over the years. Without faith, the world is a colder place, certainly, but also it can be a more optimistic one.

There are lots of suitably holy poems today, but I've decided on a secular one; Edward Thomas, writing about a confused and uncertain March such as the one which we've been experiencing, rain, hail, wind, sun, premature blooming and fading of flowers, even snow; and above it all, the urgent, passionate sound of birds just doing their own thing in spite of everything.

## March – Edward Thomas

Now I know that Spring will come again,
Perhaps to-morrow: however late I've patience
After this night following on such a day.

While still my temples ached from the cold burning
Of hail and wind, and still the primroses
Torn by the hail were covered up in it,
The sun filled earth and heaven with a great light
And a tenderness, almost warmth, where the hail dripped,
As if the mighty sun wept tears of joy.
But 'twas too late for warmth. The sunset piled
Mountains on mountains of snow and ice in the west:
Somewhere among their folds the wind was lost,
And yet 'twas cold, and though I knew that Spring
Would come again, I knew it had not come,
That it was lost too in those mountains chill.
What did the thrushes know? Rain, snow, sleet, hail,
Had kept them quiet as the primroses.
They had but an hour to sing. On boughs they sang,
On gates, on ground; they sang while they changed perches
And while they fought, if they remembered to fight:
So earnest were they to pack into that hour
Their unwilling hoard of song before the moon
Grew brighter than the clouds. Then 'twas no time
For singing merely. So they could keep off silence
And night, they cared not what they sang or screamed;

Whether 'twas hoarse or sweet or fierce or soft;
And to me all was sweet: they could do no wrong.

Something they knew – I also, while they sang
And after. Not till night had half its stars
And never a cloud, was I aware of silence
Stained with all that hour's songs, a silence
Saying that Spring returns, perhaps to-morrow

## March 31$^{st}$

Just something beautiful this morning. It comes from one of Ben Jonson's less successful comedies, *Cynthia's Revels*, written for a troop of boy actors in 1600. Jonson and Shakespeare were friends – Jonson said that he loved the man 'this side of idolatry', but they were also rivals. Responding to Heminges' and Condell's claim that Shakespeare 'never blotted a line', Jonson unwisely muttered that he wished he had 'blotted a thousand.' Later he tried to backtrack, and say that this wasn't really what he'd meant – he was simply saying that Shakespeare could write too quickly for sense. But Shakespeare must have cast a huge shadow, though for many years Jonson's reputation stood higher than that of Shakespeare. He could be coarser and cruder than Shakespeare, but he also wrote some lovely things.

Part of the play tells the story of Echo and Narcissus. Here Echo laments her fate:

> *O Narcissus,*
> *Thou that was once, and yet art, my Narcissus,*
> *Had Echo but been private with thy thoughts*
> *She would have dropt away herself in tears,*
> *Till she had all turn'd water....*

Then she sings this song, with its soft and languid musicality. It's been beautifully set to music by William Horsley (famous for the music to *There is a green hill...*).

**Slow, Slow, Fresh Fount – Ben Jonson**
Slow, slow, fresh fount, keep time with my salt tears;
    Yet, slower, yet; O faintly, gentle springs;
List to the heavy part the music bears,
    Woe weeps out her division, when she sings,
        Droop herbs and flowers,
        Fall grief and showers,
        Our beauties are not ours;
            O, I could still
    Like melting snow upon some craggy hill,
        Drop, drop, drop, drop,
Since nature's pride is now a wither'd daffodil.

# *April*

## April 4th

When we drive over the hill today, it's as though a switch has suddenly been pulled and all the glorious winter colours have been turned off – the grass is a drab olive, the bracken has faded to dull sepia, the gold to tow; everything looking as dreary as military camouflage. We've come to the end of one season, and we're waiting for another, for the summer to come to life. We wondered why Eliot described April as the 'cruellest month' – maybe he too sensed the drabness and unfinished nature of the season, the waiting for something to happen, for the lights to go on again.

I've chosen an April poem by W.H.Davies, that enigmatic and contradictory man, the 'supertramp' who was born in Wales, but who spent many years wandering around America and Canada, where he lost a leg. When he returned to England, he was befriended and supported by many people, including Edward Thomas. At times he is proudly unconventional:

> *I am the poet, Davies, William,*
> *I sin without a blush or blink,*
> *I am a man who lives to eat,*
> *I am a man who lives to drink...*

Yet his nature poetry is surprisingly delicate, so much so that D.H. Lawrence felt it was just too insubstantial. But I like this.

### April's Charms – W.H.Davies

When April scatters charms of primrose gold
Among the copper leaves in thickets old,
And singing skylarks from the meadows rise,
To twinkle like black stars in sunny skies;

When I can hear the small woodpecker ring
Time on a tree for all the birds that sing;
And hear the pleasant cuckoo, loud and long –
The simple bird that thinks two notes a song;
When I can hear the woodland brook, that could
Not drown a babe, with all his threatening mood;
Upon these banks the violets make their home,
And let a few small strawberry blossoms come:
When I go forth on such a pleasant day,
One breath outdoors takes all my cares away;
It goes like heavy smoke, when flames take hold
Of wood that's green and fill a grate with gold.

## April 6th

I like to ask friends to suggest poems to me so the choice isn't just drearily mine, and Sue Best, from the Willow Globe Theatre, has sent me a whole clutch of glorious poems, so it's hard to know what to choose first. Sue and Philip's aim is to make Shakespeare accessible, and with a mixture of professional and fine amateur players, they do just that. At the moment, they're rehearsing that mysterious, broken-backed play, *The Winter's Tale*.

I'll start with Sue's suggestion of one of Shakespeare's most beautiful sonnets, which also suits the season.

### Sonnet 98 – Wiliam Shakespeare

From you have I been absent in the spring,
When proud-pied April dress'd in all his trim
Hath put a spirit of youth in every thing,
That heavy Saturn laugh'd and leap'd with him.
Yet nor the lays of birds nor the sweet smell

Of different flowers in odour and in hue
Could make me any summer's story tell,
Or from their proud lap pluck them where they grew;
Nor did I wonder at the lily's white,
Nor praise the deep vermilion in the rose;
They were but sweet, but figures of delight,
Drawn after you, you pattern of all those.
 Yet seem'd it winter still, and, you away,
 As with your shadow I with these did play.

## April 7<sup>th</sup>

And another of Sue's poems. Robert Bridges, a fervent Christian all his life, trained as a doctor, but turned to poetry when ill health forced him to give up medicine. He became Poet Laureate, but is probably best remembered today for his support of Gerard Manley Hopkins; without him, Hopkins's poems would probably never have got published. This glorious poem tells of the power of the imagination to travel and inhabit beautiful distant landscapes.

## A Passer-by – Robert Bridges

Whither, O splendid ship, thy white sails crowding,
    Leaning across the bosom of the urgent West,
That fearest not sea rising, nor sky clouding,
    Whither away, fair rover, and what thy quest?
    Ah! soon, when Winter has all our vales opprest,
When skies are cold and misty, and hail is hurling,
    Wilt thou glide on the blue Pacific, or rest
In a summer haven asleep, thy white sails furling.

I there before thee, in the country that well thou knowest,
    Already arrived am inhaling the odorous air:
I watch thee enter unerringly where thou goest,
    And anchor queen of the strange shipping there,
    Thy sails for awnings spread, thy masts bare:
Nor is aught from the foaming reef to the snow capp'd grandest
    Peak that is over the feathery palms, more fair
Than thou, so upright, so stately and still thou standest.

And yet, O splendid ship, unhail'd and nameless,
    I know not if, aiming a fancy, I rightly divine
That thou hast a purpose joyful, a courage blameless,
    Thy port assured in a happier land than mine.
    But for all I have given thee, beauty enough is thine,
As thou, aslant with trim tackle and shrouding,
    From the proud nostril curve of a prow's line
In the offing scatterest foam, thy white sails crowding.

## April 10$^{th}$

Suffolk, where we're heading at the moment, couldn't be more different from Wales. The light in Wales is golden, Suffolk light is silver. While Wales is curves and contours, Suffolk is flat horizons and huge skies. Wales is saturated with green, Suffolk is bleached and chill. Today, Suffolk is especially beautiful in the sun, with huge swathes of creamy blackthorn blossom, and bright golden gorse.

    It's impossible to go far in south Suffolk without bumping into Benjamin Britten; his houses in Aldeburgh and Snape, the Maltings, the Maggie Hambling beach memorial, but most of all, the grey tide breaking in lacy foam on the beach, the constant hiss and roar of water on pebbles; a continual Sea Interval sounding in your head.

And as we drive through Wickham Market, the choice of music on Radio Three is a trio of Auden poems set to music by Britten; the only one I recognise is *Look, Stranger*.

As you walk the straight streets of Aldeburgh, listening to the sea and the seagulls, *Peter Grimes* is ever-present. It's hard to understand why Britten chose this strange, harsh poem by Crabbe, though he turned it into something, if not softer, at least more ambiguous. Grimes, in Crabbe's poem, is simply cruel, a man of pure evil. But the townsfolk are uncaring too – they observe Grimes's cruelty and do nothing to stop it. There is a touch of humanity about Grimes in the opera; at least the kind schoolteacher Ellen thinks so, and at times we wonder, if only briefly, whether Grimes might not have some redeeming features. His is the position of outsider in a narrow-minded society; of interest to Britten as he was living in what was then an illegal relationship with his partner. The chilling *Grimes is at his exercise* becomes part of the opera, repetitive and heartless.

### *from* Peter Grimes – George Crabbe

Peter had heard there were in London then –
Still have they being! – workhouse clearing men,
Who, undisturbed by feelings just or kind
Would parish boys to needy tradesmen bind:
They in their want a trifling sum would take,
And toiling slaves of piteous orphans make.

Such Peter sought and when a lad was found,
The sum was dealt him and the slave was bound.
Some few in town observed in Peter's trap
A boy with jacket blue and woollen cap,
But none inquired how Peter used the rope,

Or what the bruise that made the stripling stoop;
None could the ridges on his back behold,
None sought his shiv'ring in the winter's cold.
None put the question, – 'Peter, dost thou give
This boy his food? – What, man, the lad must live;
Consider, Peter, let the child have bread,
He'll serve thee better if he's stroked and fed.'
None reason'd thus – and some, on hearing cries,
Said calmly, 'Grimes is at his exercise.'

Pinn'd, beaten, cold, pinch'd, threaten'd and abused –
His efforts punished and his food refused –
Awake, tormented, and soon roused from sleep
Struck if he wept, and yet compell'd to weep....

## April 11<sup>th</sup>

Walking around the bay at Orford I remember the Auden songs we'd heard the previous day. I first read the poem *Look, Stranger* when I was at school; it was part of our O-level textbook, A Pageant of Modern Verse, as I remember. The other Auden poems were *Oh what is that sound?* and *Night Mail* – fine poems, but not ones that really gave a schoolgirl a sense of Auden. I struggled then with *Look, Stranger*; it seemed too faint, too quiet to me. Auden came back to haunt me some time later when I had an interview for the English department of a Midlands university. The interviewer asked about my reading; I said that I read poetry, which I did, and she asked me which poets I'd read. This was harder; mostly I skimmed anthologies and didn't know most poets in depth, though I probably could have blathered on a bit about Donne whom I adored. I recited a list of some poets that had cropped up in the

*Pageant;* and she immediately swooped on Auden. Auden. What did I think about Auden? Well, I'd find that quite hard to answer unprepared at 72 – at 17, I really made a hash of it. Needless to say, I didn't get the place. (The place I finally got, at London University was a bit of a hash too; I think I only got in because my Reverend Mother had made it clear in my report that she really disliked me – which luckily appealed to the eccentric professor who interviewed me.)

But although I'd found *Look, Stranger* unyielding at the time, it stayed in my head, and last year, when we had gone to Orford Ness for the day, sitting on the fragile shingle beach studded with intricate silvery sea-plants, the pale glittering sea stretching to the horizon, fragments of it were playing in my head. And now when I think of that day, I realise the scene has embedded itself in my permanent memory, just as Auden suggests. I can't print the poem, though – the Acknowledgements page at the end of the book will explain why.

## April 12th

Another favourite place in Suffolk is the Sutton Hoo burial site, where we enjoy walking through the trees imagining the great ship being dragged up from the silvery water below, to make a fitting burial site for the great king, probably Raedwald of East Anglia. I also like to think of Mrs Pretty, and her small son, living in their huge ugly house, looking out over the untouched burial mounds, in the cold misty winter days and imagining Old English warriors marching in ghostly silence through the gloom. Anyway, here to suit that mood is a snatch of Beowulf, which contains one of the most beautiful lines in Old English poetry, translated as 'The foamy-necked ship, most like a bird...' Even if you don't understand them, it's worth trying to read these lines out loud, with their seismic rhythms, their alliterations, their deep caesuras, the constant forward movement, like the boat pushed across the waves by the wind.

### *From* Beowulf (lines 210 – 218)

Fyrst forð gewat;    flota waes on yðum,
Bat under beorge.    Beornas gearwe
On stefn stigon –    streamas wundon,
Sund wið sande;    secgas baeron
On bearm nacan;    beorhte fraetwe
Guð searo geatolic;    guman ut scufon,
Weras on wilsið    wudu bundenne.
Gewat þa ofer waegholm    winde gefysed,
Flota famiheals,    fugle gelicost….

The moment had come; the ship was afloat,
Boat beneath banks. Men all prepared
Climbed into the prow, currents eddied,
Sea against sand. Men carried bright armour,
Shining weapons, into the ship's heart.
Then the heroes, on their longed-for journey,
Pushed off the planked ship
It surged over the sea, impelled by winds,
The foamy necked ship, most like a bird…

### April 15th

We come back from Suffolk via London, where we hope to meet old friends and have lunch with our family. Since we both became ill, we don't seem to spend nearly enough time in London; frequent hospital appointments (I'm not complaining; the NHS looks after us well) intrude on our free time, and usually we're only able, as now, to manage just a few days. Having lived for so many years in London, I'll always be a Londoner at heart; I love living in Wales and we have many good friends there now; but I can't lose a sneaky feeling that somehow life in London is more real. I love jumping on to a bus outside our Shoreditch flat and knowing that I'm passing the place where Milton used to live near Bunhill Fields, the burial ground where Blake and Bunyan lie, the pub where Keats grew up, and the streets through which Shakespeare hurried on his way to his theatre. I love the sense of history, how every walk takes you through layers of the deep past, meeting at ground level a modern babel of cultures and voices, everything busy, everything different.

I was amused to come across this letter, which Charles Lamb, also a passionate Londoner, had the temerity to write to Wordsworth, after a holiday in the Lakes. You can imagine the Wordsworth ladies fussing round anxiously, as he read these words, trying to soften the impact of such heresies upon their beloved.

## Charles Lamb to William Wordsworth 1801

Separate from the pleasure of your company, I don't much care if I never see another mountain in my life. I have passed all my days in London until I have formed as many and intense local attachments as any of you mountaineers can have done with dead nature. The lighted shops of the Strand and Fleet Street, the innumerable trades, tradesmen and customers, coaches, wagons, play houses, all the bustle and wickedness around Covent Garden, the very women of the town. The watchmen, drunken scenes, rattles; life awake, if you awake, at all hours of the night, the impossibility of being dull in Fleet Street, the crowds, the very dirt and mud, the sun shining upon houses and pavements, the print shops, the old book stalls, parsons cheapening books, coffee houses, steams of soup from kitchens, the pantomimes, London itself, a pantomime and masquerade, all these things work themselves into my mind and feed me without a power of satiating me. The wonder of these sights impels me into night-walks around her crowded streets and I often shed tears in the motley Strand from fullness of joy at so much life…

**April 20$^{th}$**

Back in Wales, the sun shining, the hills looking gorgeous, and kites wheeling in the sky, I feel obliged to apologise to Wordsworth, which I shall do by quoting one of his most sublime poems, and another of Sue's choices. Last time we went to Tintern Abbey, it was crowded with Japanese schoolchildren; we wondered what had brought them there, since all they were doing was taking photos of themselves, which they could just as well have done in Croydon.

If the Wordsworths hadn't ended up in the Lake District, they could very well have been associated with Wales; Wordsworth first paid a visit to Tintern Abbey in 1793 and went again in 1798. Wordsworth loved the Wye valley, and said of the wooded hillsides near the river, 'There is scarcely anything like them in the kingdom,' It was in Goodrich, near Symons Yat, that he wrote the poem *We are Seven,* having met a little girl there who gave him this reply when he asked about her family. He, along with Dorothy and Coleridge, went on a marathon walk along the Wye valley, ending up in Llyswen, nor far from Builth and from where we live. The diarist Francis Kilvert met an old man who recalled Wordsworth as a remarkable-looking man, who looked like 'an old shepherd with rough rugged weather-beaten face, but his features were fine and high cut.' He told this old man that he thought 'the Wye above Hay was the finest piece of scenery in south Britain.' It was near Llyswen that Wordsworth met the man who inspired the poem *Peter Bell*. Though this is now the busy A470, and not the quiet road that Wordsworth would have known, with peasant women carrying baskets and old men sitting outside their cottage doors, it's still a beautiful view, a soft wide valley between wooded hills on one side and the strangely striated Aberedw rocks on the other, with occasional glimpses of the broad silver blade of the Wye shining between clumps of trees. *(The hedgerows, hardly hedgerows, little lines/Of sportive wood run wild...)* Later, his wife's sister-in-law acquired a farm in Hindwell, near Old Radnor, which the Wordsworths loved, but where, tragically, they were staying when their daughter, little Catherine, died, back in Grasmere.

## *from* Lines Composed a Few Miles above Tintern Abbey – William Wordsworth

    For I have learned
To look on Nature, not as in the hour
Of thoughtless youth; but hearing oftentimes
The still sad music of humanity
Nor harsh nor grating, though of ample power
To chasten and subdue. And I have felt
A presence that disturbs me with the joy
Of elevated thoughts; a sense sublime
Of something far more deeply interfused,
Whose dwelling is the light of setting suns,
And the round ocean and the living air,
And the blue sky, and in the mind of man;
A motion and a spirit, that impels
All thinking things, all objects of all thought
And rolls through all things...

## April 23$^{rd}$

When she was small, my daughter was upset to learn that Shakespeare had died on his birthday; birthday cake and presents in the morning, the undertaker's foot on the stairs in the evening – it doesn't make for the best of days. But today everyone's celebrating 400 years since that death, and realising how important that long-dead Englishman is to all of us.

I was a little mean to Ben Jonson a few days ago, concentrating on his rivalry with, and possibly jealousy of, the other playwright. But I think Shakespeare and Jonson were good friends; one of the stories about Shakespeare's death has him dying after a fever caught when he'd had a 'merry meeting' with Jonson and Drayton. And this, from the First Folio, is one of the best, most generous, and far-seeing of all the tributes to Shakespeare.

## *From* To the Memory of My Beloved, the Author, Mr William Shakespeare – Ben Jonson

… Soul of the age!
The applause, delight, the wonder of our stage!
My Shakespeare, rise! I will not lodge thee by
Chaucer, or Spenser, or bid Beaumont lie
A little further, to make thee a room:
Thou art a monument without a tomb,
And art alive still while thy book doth live,
And we have wits to read and praise to give,
That I not mix thee so, my brain excuses,
I mean with great, but disproportion'd Muses,
For if I thought my judgement were of years,
I should commit thee surely with thy peers,
And tell how far thou dids't our Lyly outshine,
Or sporting Kyd, or Marlowe's mighty line,

And though thou had small Latin and less Greek,
From thence to honour thee I would not seek
For names; but call forth thund'ring Aeschylus,
Euripides and Sophocles to us;
Pacuvius, Accius, him of Cordova dead,
To life again, to hear thy buskin tread,
And shake a stage, or when thy socks were on,
Leave thee alone for the comparison
Of all that insolent Greece or haughty Rome
Sent forth, or did since from their ashes come.
Triumph, my Britain, thou hast one to show
To whom all scenes of Europe homage owe,
He was not for an age, but for all time!

## April 25th

Another day, another blood test. There are bad guys in the blood that have to remain stable or decrease, there are good guys that have to increase. This test is to measure the good guys so that my immune system is strong enough for me to start taking my chemo pills again; I've had to have a break from them.

How do you describe the cancer process? Are you fighting it, or not fighting? Opinions are sharply divided. I'm a non-fighter – with an incurable cancer, it would be a battle I'm bound to lose, and I don't want to feel guilty for not trying hard enough, when the battle, such as it is, is being fought out somewhere in your intestines, poisonous drugs against rogue cells. I can feel positive, or not positive, but it isn't going to affect the outcome.

Cancer comes out of nowhere, takes over and threatens to turn you into a different person. I know I'm not the person I was, and probably never will be again. But there are positive things too –

I've lost a bit of annoying middle-aged spread, I've kept my hair throughout, though I've had to let it go grey; chemo doesn't agree with hair-dye. Although I've taken loads of steroids, they haven't made my face fat, we still do most of the things we enjoy doing, though sometimes in a modified form. For most of the time, I can pass as normal; people keep telling me, a note of surprise in their voices, how well I look. I've had lots of good experiences over the last few cancer-years – we celebrated our fiftieth wedding anniversary with the people I care about most – daughters, son-in-law and grandchildren. I've written and published a book. We've travelled to Germany to see Charlemagne's treasures – a long-held ambition of mine. And as I write this, I'm still *here*.

Here's one of Emily Dickinson's oblique scrutinies on the subject of Death. Death is almost kindly and courteous, but he cannot be resisted if once he has you in his sights. The last lines hint of a belief in life-after-death, which I don't share. Or perhaps is it a suggestion that at the end of life Time slows down to a snail's pace; the equivalent of the idea that a drowning person's entire life will flash before their eyes. But there's also a suggestion that life will go on anyway, the children will still be playing in the schoolyard, whether you're there or not. And like Death in the poem, you don't mean to stop for cancer; it kindly stops for you.

**Because I could not stop for Death – Emily Dickinson**
Because I could not stop for Death
He kindly stopped for me;
The carriage held but just ourselves
And Immortality.

We slowly drove, he knew no haste,
And I had put away

My labor and my leisure too,
For his civility.
We passed the school where children strove
At recess in the ring,
We passed the fields of grazing grain,
We passed the setting sun.

We paused before a house that seemed
A swelling of the ground;
The roof was scarcely visible
The cornice but a mound.

Since then, 'tis centuries, but each
Feels shorter than the day
I first surmised the horses' heads
Were toward eternity.

## April 28$^{th}$

I looked back at my earlier poetry diary, to see what I'd posted for April 28$^{th}$ that year; the cherry blossom in London had been especially beautiful, so I'd given in to the obvious and posted Housman's famous poem. This year though, things are rather different. Blossom, when you can see it, is beautiful as ever; but the seasons have been disjointed and unpredictable; yesterday, snow, hail and sunshine all in one day, today we wake up to a heavy frost, but now pale sunshine gleams on the hills. It's the coldest April in thirty years, apparently.

As I often do, I choose a poem that's been running through my head. Christina Rossetti wrote this at twenty-seven. She would live to see many more springs, and I hope I will too. Like many of her poems, its sweetness is tinged with sadness, but not despair. Enjoy what is here now, she says, don't wait for something that might seem better. Now is all we have – don't waste it.

## Another Spring – Christina Rossetti

If I might see another Spring,
    I'd not plant summer flowers and wait;
I'd have my crocuses at once,
My leafless pink mezerons,
    My chill-veined snowdrops, choicer yet,
    My white or azure violet.
    Leaf nested primrose; anything,
    To blow at once, not late.

If I might see another Spring,
    I'd listen to the daylight birds
That build their nests and pair and sing,
Nor wait for mateless nightingale;
    I'd listen to the lusty herds,
The ewes with lambs as white as snow,
    I'd find out music in the hail
And all the winds that blow.

If I might see another Spring –
Oh stinging comments on my past,
That all my past results in 'if' –
If I might see another Spring,
I'd laugh today, today is brief,
I would not wait for anything.
    I'd use today that cannot last,
    Be glad today and sing.

# May

## May 1st

It's May Day, and I'd love to have imagery of maypoles, of girls crowned with flowers, of billowing blossom and carolling birds. Instead, in this strange weather we've been having, the sky is flat dull grey, the wind sharp, the rain threatening to turn to snow, and the trees having just started to froth with green, have now gone still and stiff again, huddling against the hedge. We had a very pleasant evening with friends last night, so we haven't yet felt the pinch of the cold and gloom, though no doubt we will as the day wears on. Hardy must have had such a May Day as this in mind when he wrote this poem. I love the 'blurting' wind and the 'pinched' buds. Shepherds are still very much in evidence, busily rounding up and moving their flocks, impervious to everything else – though the smock-frocks have long since gone, and quad-bikes and tractors accompany them and their restless, bounding dogs.

### An Unkindly May – Thomas Hardy.

A shepherd stands by a gate in a white smock-frock:
He holds the gate ajar, intently counting his flock.

The sour spring wind is blurting boisterous-wise,
And bears on it dirty clouds across the skies;
Plantation timbers creak like rusty cranes,
And pigeons and rooks, dishevelled by late rains
Are like gaunt vultures, sodden and unkempt,
And song-birds do not end what they attempt;
The buds have tried to open but quite failing
Have pinched themselves together in their quailing.

The sun frowns whitely in eye-trying flaps,
Through passing cloud-holes, mimicking audible taps.
'Nature, you're not commendable, today!'
I think. 'Better tomorrow!' she seems to say.

The shepherd still stands in that white smock-frock,
Unnoting all things save the counting his flock.

## May 5th and 6th

We seem to be having something of a Shakespeare moment – hearing that the site of the Curtain Theatre is now being excavated by the London Museum sends us on a frantic hunt to find out about a Shoreditch walk that's being advertised. But frustratingly the London Museum has decided not to answer the phone this morning, so we have to give up on that. Instead we go to an exhibition of various Shakespeare documents at Somerset House. The highlight of the exhibition is the famous will, and we see Shakespeare's signature at the end, slightly uncertain, curling up a little at the end; the current theory among scholars is that Shakespeare drafted his will perhaps a couple of years before he died, maybe suffering from a serious illness. What startles us, though, is the mention of the 'second – best bed'. This isn't part of the original will but roughly inserted between other lines, in which Shakespeare seems to hand everything over to his daughter and son-in-law. Did Anne want him to specify her ownership of this family relic, the bed in which her twins had been conceived, her children born, and which she'd occupied during those thirty years of her mysterious married life? At any rate, it seems to be a deliberate and pointed mention, rather than the casual and insensitive afterthought that it's often thought to be.

And then, the following morning, we set off on our own Shoreditch walk, to find the Curtain Theatre. We go through back streets, alleys and courtyards, still retaining the shape of the old suburb, the disreputable area of Elizabethan Shoreditch, of pubs, cheap lodging houses, small industries and scrubby market gardens, where Shakespeare lived for the first fifteen or so years of his London career, writing out his scripts in dingy lodgings, going to church with Burbage at St Leonard's, avoiding paying his taxes, obsessed with his lovely young man, and generally starting to enjoy his growing fame. This historical area can still be traced, though large chunks of it are vanishing all too fast beneath massive and impersonal blocks of glass and steel plonked over the ancient contours by greedy developers who care nothing for London.

But we find the site of the Curtain development, hidden behind hoardings, and meanly, without even a viewing window, though there are plans to preserve the remains of the playhouse beneath the flashy tent of glass walls that they plan to erect on top. Shakespeare would have divided his early days between the Curtain and the nearby theatre, and it's believed that *Henry V* and *Romeo and Juliet* were first performed here. So it's easy to imagine a play afternoon at the Curtain, the flag flying, the auditorium crowded with groundlings spitting out nutshells and gulping their beer, restless and muttering, but then, suddenly falling silent and transfixed as a beautiful boy in a tarnished rose-coloured dress, his voice still clear and light, leans out from the balcony and addresses them:

### *From* Romeo and Juliet – William Shakespeare
Come gentle night, come loving black brow'd night,
Give me my Romeo; and when he shall die
Take him and cut him out in little stars,

And he will make the face of Heaven so fine
That all the world will be in love with night…

## May 8<sup>th</sup>

A sad anniversary today – our dear friend Belinda Hollyer died a year ago. Belinda was a writer, publisher and an editor, with a personality that lit up a room and made you feel that you just had to have her for a friend. She was a great lover of poetry, and inspired me greatly when I was writing *A Bracelet of Bright Hair* – we had many exchanges about favourite poems and I was greatly enriched by them. The book was dedicated to her. It's hard to believe she's not her any more, and her bright vibrant voice still seems to echo in my mind. Sometimes, I find an old email from her, or an old Facebook post, and for a few moments, it's as if she's still here; which is why I've chosen this poem about how the dead live on with us.

### Heraclitus – William Johnson Cory
They told me, Heraclitus, they told me you were dead,
They brought be bitter news to hear and bitter tears to shed;
I wept as I remembered how often you and I
Had tired the sun with talking and sent him down the sky.

But now that thou art lying, my dear old Carian guest
A handful of grey ashes, long long ago at rest
Still are thy pleasant voices, thy nightingales awake.
For Death he taketh all away, but them he cannot take.

## May 15th

It surprises me that it's forty-five years since we first came to this mid-Wales valley. The valleys of this part of the world are very special, narrow, winding and deeply incised, and surrounded by soft hills, of an intense saturated green, scattered with dark woods. Although there have been lots of changes, the scene is still essentially as it was then; the hill that is stained crimson in the evening light, the little Clas brook tumbling noisily over bronze pebbles, the owls calling at night. The words and the accent are Border, neither Welsh nor English, and while language purists try to translate place names into acceptable Welsh, they retain their own shape and sound – Clyro, Boughrood, Erwood, Cregrina – they are like themselves and nothing else.

When we first came down with our young daughters, there were very few cars on the roads, and I'd let them wander down to the village where they'd play on the flat rocks where the river Edw flowed under the bridge. Or we'd cross a rickety bridge beneath our house and ramble alongside a little brook where watercress and yellow kingcups grew in profusion. We can't do that any more – the walk has been fenced off; and anyway today's protective mothers would be appalled by the fact that our children were allowed to roam freely near rivers. There were more pretty, decrepit cottages then, and barns like our own, which have since been tidied up and pebbledashed. Incredibly ancient shepherds stood scowling in doorways, wearing sacks tied with string over their shoulders. The quad bike hadn't arrived, and younger sons still rounded up sheep on horseback. The roadside banks were full of wild flowers, primroses and violets in the spring, stitchwort and meadowsweet, blue geraniums and red campion in the summer; there are still flowers, but the profusion has gone. We used to have buzzards wheeling overhead; now they're more likely to be red kites – of which we have a pair nesting in the next field. Now the beautiful valley has acquired a couple of intrusive wind turbines and there are threats of a huge industrial chicken farm being built within scenting-distance. Redbrick bungalows have sprung up, but bringing with them such nice neighbours that we don't mind.

I remember all those years ago when our daughters were exclaiming, as little girls do, at the baby lambs and how sweet they were. We had a rather unkind friend staying with us at the time, who hadn't yet had children and didn't get how it worked, who tried to upset our girls for their 'sentimentality' by sneerily muttering 'Sunday lunch' and 'mint sauce' at them. Fortunately my daughters didn't seem to be distressed at this, and simply decided that this was not a person they had to like.

It was about this time, I think, that we came across these two lambs, mysteriously dead, in a stream, and I wrote this poem, which I've just uncovered in a drawer of ancient stuff.

**Seasonal**
Curled in the stream's crook, the children found them,
and mourned for death. Something – a fox, perhaps,
had got them first, peeled back the fleece
so all the glistening purple showed, veined like a map.
The survivors, meanwhile, played and gambolled,
danced out their fragile time of grace,
as the children gave them names and tried to stroke them.
The season's numbness bit to the bone
all but the strong and green. Cold had compacted
earth, stone. The flooded waters roared.

In summer we came back. Not a trace
of those two dead ones, not a rib, a skull.

Meadowsweet creamed at the margins, bracken lay over the hill.
The other lambs too had vanished. Some I suppose
had stupefied into sheep. For the rest... well... for a bit
butchers were places we walked quickly past...
The children, anyway, forgot. There was a badger dead on the road.
Soon it blew up and stank. They found a caterpillar for a pet.
This year the blackberries come slowly
I hope they ripen soon. In August, the hedgecutter comes.

## May 16<sup>th</sup>

Well, it does seem that summer is finally here, after our long, cold spring. The cuckoo is calling from the woods opposite and house martins are flashing their white breasts as they dart in and out of their nest under the eaves. Trees have finally exploded into leaf, and the hedges are weighed down by creamy dollops of hawthorn flowers. Driving back through Herefordshire yesterday we saw all the cider apple orchards starry with blossom. It's a happy time for us now, just as it was for the poets of the Middle Ages, emerging from the long dark winter. It's hard to beat the simple burst of joy of this song from the thirteenth century, intended to be sung as a round. (Llouth seems to be a cow, verteth is - um- farteth).

## Sumer is icumen in – Anonymous

Sumer is icumen in,
Lhude sing cuccu!
Groweth sed and bloweth med
And springth the wode nu,
Sing cuccu!
Awe bleteth after lomb,
Lhouth after calue cu.

Bulluc sterteth, bucke uerteth,
Murie sing cuccu!
Cuccu, cuccu, wel singes thu cuccu;
Ne swik thu nauer nu.
Sing cuccu nu. Sing cuccu.
Sing cuccu. Sing cuccu nu!

## May 18th

I've been pleased to have this poem sent to me by my friend the writer Jane Stemp, who has a fine ear for poetry and seems to find lovely ones that I don't know. For some reason, I'd overlooked this by Herbert, though it's sitting there in my Collected Poems of George Herbert.

### Prayer – George Herbert

Prayer the Churches banquet, Angels age,
    Gods breath in man returning to his birth
    The soul in paraphrase, heart in pilgrimage,
The Christian plummet sounding heav'n and earth;

Engine against th'Almightie, sinners towre,
    Reversed thunder, Christ-side-piercing spear,
    The six-daies – world transposing in an houre,
A kinde of tune, which all things heare and fear;

Softnesse, and peace, and joy, and love, and blisse,
    Exalted Manna, gladnesse of the best,
    Heaven in ordinarie, man well drest,
The milkie may, the bird of Paradise,
    Church-bells beyond the stares heard, the souls bloud,
    The land of spices; something understood.

## May 19th

The most beautiful thing in our garden at the moment must be the crab apple tree on the lawn. I planted it some years ago, to replace a much-loved hundred-year old tree which had finally split in two. It has pretty golden crabs in the autumn, or it should do, but up till now, it's always been rather straggly and sparse, not really deserving its central place on our lawn. But this year, a year of blossom, it's come into its own, and is laden thickly with a mass of blush-pink flowers, like Samuel Palmer's Magic Apple Tree.

The poem running through my head is this, by William Barnes. Richard used to sing it in the famous setting by Vaughan Williams. But it was tidied up for the music and rewritten in standard English. I don't normally like poems in dialect, but this is how Barnes originally wrote it. We visited the site of Barnes's cottage when we were in Dorset a few years ago, after following the much better known Hardy trail. Barnes was born into a poor family, became a clerk and then, later on, after his marriage to Julia, the love of his life, a clergyman. As well as being a poet, he was also a talented artist and engraver, and known for being tireless in carrying out his parish duties. He died in 1886, in his parish of Winterborne Came.

## Linden Lea – William Barnes

'Ithin the woodlands, flow'ry gleaded,
By the woak tree's mossy moot,
The sheenen grass-bleades, timber-sheaded,
Now do quiver under voot ;
An' birds do whissle over head,
An' water's bubblen in its bed,
An' there vor me the apple tree
Do lean down low in Linden Lea.
When leaves that leately wer a-springen

Now do feade 'ithin the copse,
An' painted birds do hush their zingen
Up upon the timber's tops;
An' brown-leav'd fruit's a turnen red,
In cloudless zunsheen, over head,
Wi' fruit vor me, the apple tree
Do lean down low in Linden Lea.
Let other vo'k meake money vaster
In the air o' dark-room'd towns,
I don't dread a peevish measter;
Though noo man do heed my frowns,
I be free to goo abrode,
Or teake agean my hwomeward road
To where, vor me, the apple tree
Do lean down low in Linden Lea.

## May 20<sup>th</sup>

I suppose Barnes was trying to give an authentic voice to people who would otherwise be silent and invisible, but the heavy dialect does get in the way of enjoyment. Poetry has a visual, as well as an auditory appeal; some lines appeal as much to the eye as to the ear: *'Sandalwood, cedarwood and sweet white wine…' 'My heart is like a singing bird…' 'The silver apples of the moon…'* The words *look* lovely upon the page, before you even hear them. But dialect poems have to be translated, and you're deprived of that visual pleasure. Sometimes, as with Scots poets, there's a political element about the use of dialect; modern rap verse, which I don't know anything about, strives to create an authentic black working-class sound. And I have a suspicion that dialect can hide a banality of thought. Dylan Thomas, in *Under Milk Wood* manages to create a language that has the rhythms and sounds of Welsh without concealing the words in dialect – it can be done.

My friend Jane has sent me poems by a favourite of hers, William Soutar. Soutar (1898-1943) was a Scotsman who suffered from ill health all his life, though he spent two years in the navy in World War One. After the war, he turned to poetry, and wrote much of it in Scots dialect, which I find impenetrable. But Jane, knowing my dislike of Scots poetry, has sent this in standard English, a moving lament for friends lost in the war.

**The Permanence of the Young Men – William Soutar**
No man outlives the grief of war
Though he outlive its wreck:
Upon the memory a scar
Through all his years will ache.

Hopes will revive when horrors cease;
And dreaming dread be stilled;
But there shall dwell within his peace
A sadness unannulled.

Upon his world shall hang a sign
Which summer cannot hide:
The permanence of the young men
Who are not by his side.

**May 22$^{nd}$**
I wanted to post a poem today, but lacking inspiration I turned to a poetry site on the web, and found this, new to me, as a Poem of the Day. And since I've been thinking about Scots poetry, this, by

William Dunbar, seemed fortuitously right. Dunbar was a poet at the court of King James IV of Scotland, at the end of the fifteenth and beginning of the sixteenth century, a time when not many poets were writing south of the border. His language, in the original manuscripts, echoes Scots pronunciations, not because he's consciously writing in dialect, but because standard English hadn't really happened, and wouldn't do so until the following century and the growth in popular printing. (This version has been modernised and Englished.) I like this poem because, although the theme of the cruel mistress isn't original, there's a crystalline purity and elegance about the language, a slow and graceful languor to the rhythm, and the intricate flower imagery is exquisitely done.

## Sweet Rose of Virtue – William Dunbar

Sweet rose of virtue and of gentleness,
delightful lily of youthful wantonness,
richest in bounty and in beauty clear
and in every virtue that is held most dear —
except only that you are merciless.

Into your garden, today, I followed you;
there I saw flowers of freshest hue,
both white and red, delightful to see,
and wholesome herbs, waving resplendently —
yet nowhere, one leaf or flower of rue.

I fear that March with his last arctic blast
has slain my fair rose of pallid and gentle cast,
whose piteous death does my heart such pain
that, if I could, I would compose her roots again —
so comforting her bowering leaves have been.

## May 23rd

Ollie, next door's fat ginger cat, is sitting very still and patiently in the long grass under the tree waiting for some hapless small creature to emerge. Unfortunately, he doesn't realise that ginger and bright green is a lousy colour combination for camouflage, and the small creatures are keeping quiet.

Alas, we don't have any cats at the moment, though we've had some lovely ones in the past. I'm not a dog lover; I find dogs hyperactive and demanding, giving their owners endless trouble; but a house without a cat always seems incomplete to me. When I was a child, and a kindly nun (there were a few) told me that in Heaven you could have anything you wanted, I used to imagine that I would be reunited with lost cats there. It still seems like something which could make Heaven a more interesting place; Rufus, Archy, Minnie, Sarah, Hodge; I'd love to meet up with you all again.

Here's one of my favourite bits of cat poetry, a fragment by Matthew Arnold. Did he like cats or not? Hard to tell from this, but I hope he did.

### *From* Poor Matthias – Matthew Arnold

Cruel, but composed and bland,
Dumb, inscrutable and grand,
So Tiberius might have sat,
Had Tiberius been a cat.

## May 24th

Today is a tidying-up my study day, and as always I'll do anything to avoid getting started on this task. A poetry diary becomes a good excuse ('I can't *possibly* start tidying up until I've finished my diary.')

But it has to be done by Friday as granddaughter will be sleeping on the Put-u-up, and will expect to find 'her bedroom' in order. I'm an untidy person – always have been – and my study is in a state of chaos and confusion. Chaos and confusion – this surely calls for Milton and Hell. Satan, after a discussion with his fellow devils about the best way of getting back at God, decides to approach His new creation, Man. Satan leaves the fearful dungeon of Hell, and steps out into Chaos, where the four elements are still warring for balance, and still managing to achieve nothing but more chaos. Not too much unlike my study, then.

### *From* Paradise Lost Bk II – John Milton
Before thir eyes in sudden view appear
The secrets of the hoarie deep, a dark
Illimitable Ocean without bound,
Without dimension, where length, breadth, and higtht
And time and place are lost: where eldest Night
And *Chaos,* Ancestors of Nature, hold
Eternal *Anarchie,* amidst the noise
Of endless warrs, and by confusion stand.
For hot, cold moist and dry, four Champions fierce
Strive here for Maistrie, and to Battel bring
Thir embryon Atoms; they around the flag
Of each his faction, in thir several Clans,
Light-arm'd or heavy, sharp, smooth, swift, or slow,
Swarm populous, unnumber'd as the sands
Of Barca or Cyrene's torrid soil,
Levied to side with warring Winds, and poise
Their lighter wings. To whom thee most adhere
Hee rules a moment; *Chaos* umpire sits
And by decision more imbroiles the fray

By which he Reigns; next him, high Arbiter
*Chance* governs all. Into this wilde Abyss,
The womb of nature and perhaps her Grave,
Of neither Sea, nor Shore, nor Air, nor Fire,
But all these in thir pregnant causes mixt
Confusedly, and which thus must ever fight,
Unless th'Almighty Maker them ordain
His dark materials to create more Worlds…

## May 27th

Today is the feast day of St Melangell; one of the more charming of Welsh saints. She was an Irish princess who fled her homeland to avoid an arranged marriage and came to a lovely valley near Bala (now called Pennant Melangell.) A local prince and his retinue were hunting the hare; they burst into a clearing in the valley to find Melangell sheltering the hare beneath her skirts, and the hounds drew back from her. The prince was so impressed that he gave her the valley for her own and she built a church and a nunnery there. She's now the patron saint of hares. The church still stands, with Melangell's shrine inside, reconstituted from fragments rebuilt into the wall. It's a magic place, a 'thin place' as Christians say, where the membrane between heaven and earth seems to be stretched fine. It's become a place of healing, and now houses a centre for cancer sufferers.

The hare poem that comes to mind is this, by William Cowper. Cowper kept two hares as pets, Puss and Tiney, and though the thought of keeping hares as pets makes modern blood run cold, he was a good and affectionate master, and perhaps having animals to love helped stave off the shattering depressions to which he was prone. As in his letters, which someone described as 'divine table talk', and which are one of my favourite bedtime readings, the charm lies in the attention to little domestic details, the Turkey carpet, the foods that made up Tiney's diet, his bad temper. Though Tiney doesn't seem to have been too happy, he was obviously well-looked after and loved. And as always with Cowper, there's a touch of unreachable melancholy; he mourns not only Tiney's death, but looks ahead to the time when his other pet hare will die too.

**Epitaph on a Hare – William Cowper**
Here lies, whom hound did ne'er pursue,
Nor swifter greyhound follow,
Whose foot ne'er tainted morning dew,
Nor ear heard huntsman's halloo',
Old Tiney, surliest of his kind,
Who, nursed with tender care,
And to domestic bounds confined,
Was still a wild jack-hare.
Though duly from my hand he took
His pittance every night,
He did it with a jealous look,
And, when he could, would bite.
His diet was of wheaten bread,
And milk, and oats, and straw,
Thistles, or lettuces instead,
With sand to scour his maw.
On twigs of hawthorn he regaled,
On pippins' russet peel;
And, when his juicy salads failed,
Sliced carrot pleased him well.
A Turkey carpet was his lawn,

Whereon he loved to bound,
To skip and gambol like a fawn,
And swing his rump around.

His frisking was at evening hours,
For then he lost his fear;
But most before approaching showers,
Or when a storm drew near.

Eight years and five round-rolling moons
He thus saw steal away,
Dozing out his idle noons,
And every night at play.

I kept him for his humour's sake,
For he would oft beguile
My heart of thoughts that made it ache,
And force me to a smile.

But now, beneath this walnut-shade
He finds his long, last home,
And waits in snug concealment laid,
Till gentler Puss shall come.

He, still more aged, feels the shocks
From which no care can save,
And, partner once of Tiney's box,
Must soon partake his grave.

## May 28<sup>th</sup>

Thinking of William Cowper sent me back to his letters, where I found this delightful description of his summer house and writing retreat; hard to realise from this that he was subject often to violent fits of depression and religious despair.

## Letter to Joseph Hill, 1785 – William Cowper

... I write in a nook that I call my Boudoir. It is a summer house not much bigger than a sedan-chair, the door of which opens into the garden, that is now crowded with pinks, roses and honeysuckles, and the window into my neighbour's orchard. It formerly served an apothecary, now dead, as a smoking room; and under my feet is a trapdoor, which once covered a hole in the ground, where he kept his bottles. At present, however, it is dedicated to sublimer uses. Having lined it with garden mats, and furnished it with a table and two chairs, here I write all that I write in summer-time, whether to my friends, or to the public. It is secure from all noise, and refuge from all intrusion; for intruders sometimes trouble me in the winter evenings at Olney. But (thanks to my Boudoir!) I can now hide myself from them. A poet's retreat is sacred.

## May 29th

May, the month and the blossom will soon be over. It's been an amazing year for may, or hawthorn blossom; hedges bubbling over with creamy flowers, the banks a white haze of cow-parsley, the air full of honey-sweet but pungent scent. Driving down the road is like going through an endless bridal procession.

Hawthorn of course, brings Proust to mind; for him it was as much a memory trigger as the more famous madeleines. The sensitive boy was ravished by the blossoms which he saw as he walked along Swann's Way and which decorated the church. He had a minutely observant eye for the delicate details of the flowers, which he describes exquisitely; the little cluster of stamens, the creamy, freckled spots. But alas, soon these beautiful things would become poisonous to him, as they brought on the asthma which crippled him.

## *From* Swann's Way – Marcel Proust (Scott Moncrieff translation)

It was in these 'Month of Mary' services that I can remember having first fallen in love with hawthorn-blossom. The hawthorn was not merely in the church, for there, holy ground as it was, we had all of us a right of entry; but, arranged upon the altar itself, inseparable from the mysteries in whose celebration it was playing a part, it thrust in among the tapers and the sacred vessels its rows of branches, tied to one another horizontally in a stiff, festal scheme of decoration; and they were made more lovely still by the scalloped outline of the dark leaves, over which were scattered in profusion, as over a bridal train, little clusters of buds of a dazzling whiteness. Though I dared not look at them save through my fingers, I could feel that the formal scheme was composed of living things, and that it was Nature herself who, by trimming the shape of the foliage, and by adding the crowning ornament of those snowy buds, had made the decorations worthy of what was at once a public rejoicing and a solemn mystery. Higher up on the altar, a flower had opened here and there with a careless grace, holding so unconcernedly, like a final, almost vaporous bedizening, its bunch of stamens, slender as gossamer, which clouded the flower itself in a white mist...

...When, before turning to leave the church, I made a genuflection before the altar, I felt suddenly, as I rose again, a bitter-sweet fragrance of almonds steal towards me from the hawthorn-blossom, and I then noticed that on the flowers themselves were little spots of a creamier colour, in which I imagined that this fragrance must lie concealed, as the taste of an almond cake lay in the burned parts, or the sweetness of Mlle. Vinteuil's cheeks beneath their freckles. Despite the heavy, motionless silence of the hawthorns, these gusts of fragrance came to me like the murmuring of an intense vitality, with which the whole altar was quivering like a roadside hedge explored by living antennae, of which I was reminded by seeing some stamens, almost red in colour, which seemed to have kept the springtime virulence, the irritant power of stinging insects now transmuted into flowers.

## May 30th

With the grandchildren on the motorway on their way to see us, my book opened by a nice chance upon this extract from John Clare's *Shepherd's Calendar*. Clare (1793 -1864) is one of the sadder figures in English poetry. He was born into the family of a poor labourer near Peterborough. At first his poetry brought him money and fame, but the success didn't last, and the stress of trying to care for his wife and seven children triggered a breakdown, and he passed the last years of his life in an asylum. Recently an unpleasant copyright dispute has meant that many of his finer poems are no longer available to the public – especially sad that after all his difficulties his voice is effectively silenced again.

Clare isn't just a rude peasant poet; like Proust, he has an extraordinary sensitivity to details, and to getting inside the minds and feelings of the characters in his poems. The details here – the picture-pasted screen, the shadows on the wall, the ladder to the attic, bring this evening scene vividly alive, and we share the children's feelings of horror and fascination at the grandmother's scary tales. This evening, we were talking about the film of Roald Dahl's story *The Witches*, and four-year-old Jacob took it into his head that witches might come into his bedroom. However much you try to assure children that there is nothing lurking under the bed or behind the cupboard door, you can never quite chase away that fear.

### *From* January – The Shepherd's Calendar – John Clare
Thus dame the winter-night regales
With wonders never ceasing tales;
While in a corner, ill at ease,
Or crushing twixt their father's knees,
The children – silent all the while –
And een repressed the laugh or smile-
Quake with the ague chills of fear,
And tremble though they love to hear;
Starting, while they the tales recall,
At their own shadows on the wall;
Thill the old clock that strikes unseen
Behind the picture-pasted screen
Where Eve and Adam still agree
To rob Life's fatal apple-tree
Counts over bed-times hour of rest,
And bids each be sleep's fearful guest.
She then her half-told tales will leave
To finish on to-morrow's eve –
The children steal away to bed,
And up the ladder softly tread;
Scarce daring – from their fearful joys
To look behind or make a noise...

# *June*

## June 1st

Half way through the year, and we've had a beautiful week of sunshine. I'm in much better shape than I was in January, and enjoying the warmth and the flowers. The two kites nesting in the opposite field have beome three; we have heard a nearby cuckoo, and house martins are swooping about. Roses aren't out yet, but columbine, yellow welsh poppies, geraniums and honeysuckle are in full bloom. The feathery leaves of the tall fennel make a green mist, fruit is ripening on the gooseberry bushes. Yesterday the children were excited to see metallic blue dragonflies in a field awash with daisies and buttercups. Bumble bees are humming everywhere and nosing into flowers. Once again, I look to John Clare. While Wordsworth is always regarded as our greatest poet of nature, his eye is always on the grand and sublime; when he sinks to detail, he can be banal, as in his ode to the celandine. But Clare observes the smallest things with painstaking care, and transforms them into beauty – the glittering haze of insects, the streaked woodbine, the spiders' webs like wet fairy dresses. Here he is with a wonderfully evocative piece about June.

## *From* June – The Shepherd's Calendar – John Clare

Now summer is in flower and nature's hum
Is never silent round her sultry bloom
Insects as small as dust are never done
Wi' glittering dance and reeling in the sun
And green wood fly and blossom haunting bee
Are never weary of their melody
Round field hedge now flowers in full glory twine

Large bindweed bells wild hop and streakd woodbine
That lift athirst their slender throated flowers
Agape for dew falls and for honey showers
These round each bush in sweet disorder run
And spread their wild hues to the sultry sun
Where its silk netting lace on twigs and leaves
The mottld spider at eves leisure weaves
That every morning meet the poets eye
Like faireys dew wet dresses hung to dry
The wheat swells into ear and leaves below
The may month wild flowers and their gaudy show
Bright carlock bluecap and corn poppy red
Which in such clouds of colors widely spread
That at the sun rise might to fancys eye
Seem to reflect the many colord sky
And leverets seat and lark and partridge nest…

## June 3rd

Yet though June is beautiful, the world is still in a mess. Isis spews out its propaganda of hate; Donald Trump is slouching inexorably towards Washington, and thanks to David Cameron's foolish decision to hold a referendum, there's a real danger that a gang of unsavoury men is going to persuade us to leave the EU, which could surely be one of the stupidest moves of this century. The ghastly war in Syria continues, and there is still no answer to the refugee problem. Rudyard Kipling writes of a similar period of despair and desolation at the end of the First World War, in which he lost a son. Justice is needed, but how can it ever emerge from such confusion?

# Justice – Rudyard Kipling

Across a world where all men grieve
And grieving strive the more,
The great days range like tides and leave
Our dead on every shore.
Heavy the load we undergo,
And our own hands prepare,
If we have parley with the foe,
The load our sons must bear.

Before we loose the word
That bids new worlds to birth,
Needs must we loosen first the sword
Of Justice upon earth;
Or else all else is vain
Since life on earth began,
And the spent world sinks back again
Hopeless of God and Man.

A People and their King
Through ancient sin grown strong,
Because they feared no reckoning
Would set no bound to wrong;
But now their hour is past,
And we who bore it find
Evil Incarnate hell at last
To answer to mankind.

For agony and spoil
Of nations beat to dust,
For poisoned air and tortured soil
And cold, commanded lust,

And every secret woe
The shuddering waters saw.
Willed and fulfilled by high and low.
Let them relearn the Low.

That when the dooms are read,
Not high nor low shall say:-
'My haughty or my humble head
Was saved me in this day.'
That, till the end of time,
Their remnant shall recall
Their fathers old, confederate crime
Availed them not at all.

That neither schools nor priests,
Nor Kings may build again
A people with the heart of beasts
Made wise concerning men.
Whereby our dead shall sleep
In honour, unbetrayed,
And we in faith and honour keep
That peace for which they paid.

## June 4th

Oh dear – a cheerful note is needed now. And as we're going to a wedding party this evening, that should do the trick. Still, I hope, enjoying this gorgeous weather, we'll be driving across the Cambrian mountains, to Aberystwyth and the sea, and to the austere grey Georgian mansion, Nanteos, ('nightingale stream') set in quiet woods and parkland; famous for keeping the Holy Grail supposedly tucked away in a cupboard somewhere. Here's a little poem by the Scottish poet, James Thomson, which will serve nicely for a wedding banquet. And I hope we hear those nightingales.

**The Wine of Love – James Thomson**
The wine of Love is music,
    And the feast of Love is song,
And when Love sits down to the banquet,
    Love is long.

Sits long and arises drunken,
    But not with the feast and the wine,
He reeleth with his own heart,
    That great rich Vine.

**June 5th**

We go for a walk upon one of our quiet, lonely hills this morning, something I haven't done for ages because of laziness, bad weather and grumbling bones. But today the sun is shining brightly though the hills are hidden in a misty haze, my back feels strong, and I'm able to stride at almost my old pace. We see curlews, kites, and hear hundreds of larks, their warbling filling the air. A hare bounds across our path and vanishes. Little orange tip butterflies flutter among the heather, and the wild bilberries (the best pies on the planet) grow in acid green-yellow tussocks everywhere. New bracken leaves unfurl their croziers, tiny yellow buttercups – whose name I ought to know, but can't remember, are scattered everywhere. The walk was certainly worth it.

    The lonely cry of the curlew brings to mind this poem by W.B. Yeats – at first sight a little too full of the fey misty images of his early poems, but there's something strangely evocative about it, something that stays in the mind. (Curlews *and* peewits, though?) Echtge seems to be a mountain range in Ireland.

## The Withering of the Boughs – W.B.Yeats

I cried when the moon was murmuring to the birds:
'Let peewit call and curlew cry where they will,
I long for your merry and tender and pitiful words,
For the roads are unending, and there is no place to my mind.'
The honey-pale moon lay low on the sleepy hill,
And I fell asleep upon lonely Echtge of streams.
*No boughs have withered because of the wintry wind;*
*The boughs have withered because I have told them my dreams.*

I know of the leafy paths that the witches take
Who come with their crowns of pearl and their spindles of wool,
And their secret smile, out of the depths of the lake;
I know where a dim moon drifts, where the Danaan kind
Wind and unwind their dances when the light grows cool
On the island lawns, their feet where the pale foam gleams.
*No boughs have withered because of the wintry wind;*
*The boughs have withered because I have told them my dreams.*

I know of the sleepy country, where swans fly round
Coupled with golden chains, and sing as they fly.
A king and a queen are wandering there, and the sound
Has made them so happy and hopeless, so deaf and so blind
With wisdom, they wander till all the years have gone by;
I know, and the curlew and peewit on Echtge of streams.
*No boughs have withered because of the wintry wind;*
*The boughs have withered because I have told them my dreams.*

## June 6th

Partly due to steroids – beastly things – I've had various eye problems, including cataracts. One eye has already been operated on, and I'm due to have the other next week. One thing is worrying me. Through the operated-on eye, everything is much brighter, whiter, clearer, almost bleached. Trouble is, when I look at sunsets, they get bleached too, almost to white. Through my 'bad' eye, which my optician says is so occluded he's surprised I can see anything, I can still get the full pink-and-gold impact of the sunset. The eye surgeon regards my question about this as so stupid, he doesn't even deign to answer it. My granddaughter asks, rather intelligently, if I can still see sunsets in photographs – which I can – it's just the real thing which eludes me. Am I going to lose sunsets after next week? In Wales, the colours gather slowly in the cup of our valley, intensify and then seep along the lines of the hills, colouring the whole valley. In London, even more spectacularly, streaks of pink reflect back from all the windows of our block of flats, doubling and tripling the impact of the glow, and polishing the surrounding walls to silver. A sunset-free world seems rather a desolate one. Well, I shall have to wait till Friday week.

I can't find any poems I like about sunsets. A haiku seems appropriate, so for the first time I've had a go at one.

## Sunset

This gift from evening,
Rose-pink, gold, drenching the sky,
Drowns us in glory.

## June 9th

One of the incidental pleasures about this poetry diary is the way in which poems can sometimes come suddenly out of the blue, landing on what would, in the old days, have been your polished walnut desk, though today it's likely to be a cyberhole in your computer. This morning, when I woke up, I berated myself for a lack of ideas. I didn't want to keep writing about the weather, and the routine of a trip to Tesco, watering the garden and sorting out the washing, offered nothing in the way of inspiration. And then I opened my email, and there from Jane, was the file she'd promised to send me, full of her lovely poems. She's agreed that I can use one in this diary – hard to choose, but I loved this.

### Weathermaps – Jane Stemp

**1: frozen in**
Yesterday outside,
webs dewbound and frozen -
how the icebeads trembled
under the feet of air.

Caught under the glass
lie rings and necklaces and
small leaflight shapes of gold
that quiver at our tread;

history like a spider
feels us passing by.

**2: counting raincoats**
Under the streetlamps couples
move dancing to fend off the rain

hands over heads
in ritual beige raincoats.
We have no protection
against the unexpected.

Beyond the glass a man
patiently cleans his car;
with one hand
and a sodden bap of tissues
he strokes the running dirt
down the sleek curves.
No sentries to alert us
to the unguarded word.

Nothing to be done
but anyway let us live
and not be sorry
for an hour spent holding hands
and counting raincoats.

## 3: fogbound

Lights blossom in the fog that hangs
like twilight through the day.
This guess from hue to hue,
is it the feel of colourblind,
was it this shifting dim to dark
that made our Saxon ancestors
call colour by shades of light?
Burnished, sallow, bright and wan;
strings of intensities that help
the colourblind choose pictures and see
lights blossom in the fog.

## 4: winter sunlight

Three things I want to touch;
the sharp bone at the outside of your wrist,
the back of children's necks,
the hollow between the shoulderblades of cats
sitting upright to be stroked.
These three things make me ache
and a fourth is a winter day
where light strikes light, slanting
through glass like frozen sunshine.
So fragile it is, a wonder
it shines at all: shadows
lie tender on the ground,
ready to blow away.
Shadows and cats and youth
how light they leave us,
but chiselled on my mind
the look of your hands
and that sharp bone.


## June 12th

This afternoon, we intend to go to one of my favourite gardens, Bryans Ground, near Presteigne. It's a beautiful confection of architectural perfection- alleys and courts and waterways and clipped yews – and blousy exuberance of rampaging self seeded and overflowing geraniums and roses and feathery wild fennel. There's a yellow path, a pink, a deep red – but all subtle, never garish. Surprises and gentle jokes assail you at every turn; little passages slip between hedges and deliver you into different worlds, irises banked like an army, sinuous water gardens, views through to meadows where horses graze; espaliered apple trees clasp beds of beans and cabbages; watering cans and spades lurk everywhere in carefully crafted patterns. There are rooms and gazebos in which to hide and sulk, benches to survey distant views, and sinuous paths mown through wild grasses. Marvell's Garden poem, one of my favourites when I was younger, seems to fit here. Marvell, that enigmatic and puzzling poet of the seventeenth century, suggests that his idea of paradise is a solitary one, spent in a beautifully ordered garden.

## The Garden – Andrew Marvell

How vainly men themselves amaze
To win the Palm, the Oke, the Bayes;
And their uncessant Labours see
Crown'd from some single Herb or Tree.
Whose short and narrow verged Shade
Does prudently their Toyles upbraid;
While all Flow'rs and all Trees do close
To weave the Garlands of repose.

Fair quiet, have I found thee here,
And Innocence thy Sister dear!
Mistaken long, I sought you then
In busie Companies of Men,
Your sacred plants, if here below,
Only among the Plants will grow.
Society is all but rude
To this delicious Solitude.

No white nor red was ever seen
So am'rous as this lovely green.
Fond lovers, cruel as their Flame,
Cut in these trees their Mistress name.
Little, Alas, they know or heed,
How far these Beauties Hers exceed!
Fair Trees! Where s'eer your barkes I wound,
No name shall but your own be found.

When we have run our Passions heat,
Love hither makes his best retreat.
The *Gods* that mortal Beauty chase
Still in a Tree did end their race.
*Apollo* hunted *Daphne* so
Only that She might Laurel grow.
And *Pan* did after *Syrinx* speed,
Not as a Nymph but for a Reed.

What wond'rous Life is this I lead!
Ripe Apples drop about my head;
The Luscious Clusters of the Vine
Upon my Mouth do crush their Wine;
The Nectarene, and curious Peach
Into my hands themselves do reach;
Stumbling on Melons as I pass,
Insnar'd with Flow'rs, I fall on Grass.

Mean while the Mind, from pleasure less,
Withdraws into its happiness:
The Mind, that Ocean where each kind
Does straight its own resemblance find;

Yet it creates, transcending these,
Far other Worlds, and other Seas;
Annihilating all that's made
To a green Thought in a green Shade.

Here at the Fountains sliding foot,
Or at some Fruit-trees mossy root,
Casting the Bodies Vest aside,
My Soul into the boughs does glide:
There like a Bird, it sits and sings,
Then whets and combs its silver Wings;
And till prepar'd for longer flight,
Waves in its Plumes the various Light.

Such was that happy Garden-state,
While Man there walked without a Mate:
After a Place so pure and sweet,
What other Help could yet be meet!
But 'twas beyond a Mortal's share
To wander solitary there;
Two Paradises 'twere in one
To live in Paradise alone.

How well the skilful Gardner drew
Of flow'rs and herbes this Dial new:
Where from above the milder Sun
Does through a fragrant Zodiack run;
And as it works, th'industrious Bee
Computes its time as well as we.
How could such sweet and wholsome Hours
Be reckon'd but with herbs and flow'rs!

## June 13th

After the terrible massacre in the gay nightclub in Orlando, and the rush of homophobia and racism which has followed it, poetry seems somehow inappropriate. And once more, we think about the stupidity of a country which allows – even seems to encourage – deranged men to buy automatic weapons, suitable only for mass murder. But I'll post this little elegy by Edward Thomas for young men who will never see their homes and loved ones again.

### In Memoriam – Edward Thomas
The flowers left thick at nightfall in the wood
This Eastertide call into mind the men,
Now far from home, who, with their sweethearts, should
Have gathered them and will do never again

## June 14th

Prayer, especially for an agnostic, seems a strange instinct; throwing words into the air where there may be nothing to receive them. Yet it's an embedded instinct; most people under intense pressure would send up a prayer – *please make it stop, please don't let it happen*. I was thinking again of those poor creatures in Orlando awaiting death from the deranged gunman slowly and lethally stalking them – surely most of them would have sent up prayers as they heard those deadly footsteps coming closer.

And there's something special about places where prayers have been sent up for generations; it's why we love going to our little thirteenth-century church of St David's, though alas, the Church in Wales seems to regard such places as irrelevant nowadays. Why sit in a stone church that needs upkeep when you can do just as well in a village hall? But it's impossible to sit in our church with its carved rood-screen without wondering about the others who have stood there over the centuries, some praying fervently, others just anxious to be let out, and the intricate web of sacred language and song that's been woven there.

Last year, we went to Southwark Cathedral, and there found the tomb of Lancelot Andrewes. Andrewes, an intensely learned man, ended his days as Bishop of Winchester. He was famous for his sermons, less well known, but just as magnificent, as those of Donne. And those who wonder why the language of the King James' Bible is so beautiful must know that Andrewes was one of those who compiled it – it wasn't just a group of faceless bureaucrats, but some of the best writers of the day. He wrote many prayers for private devotion; this we found transcribed on his grave.

**Prayer – Lancelot Andrews**
Thou, O Lord, art the helper of the helpless, the hope of the hopeless, the saviour of them who are tossed with the tempests, the haven of them who sail. Be thou all to all. The glorious majesty of the Lord our God be upon us. Oh, prosper thou our handiwork, Lord. Be thou within us to strengthen us, without us to keep us, above us to protect us, beneath us, to strengthen us, before us to direct us, behind us to keep us from straying, round about us, to defend us. Blessed be thou, O Lord our Father for ever and ever.

**June 16$^{th}$**
What with Marvell and Andrewes, I find myself still hovering around the seventeenth century, not a bad place to be when it comes to poetry, especially as the great British public seems to be making a lemming-like rush towards leaving the EU. Outside, even

our summer seems to have deserted us for teeming rain, and I have to go and have my cataract operation tomorrow. And at the end of the day, we hear of the horrific murder of Jo Cox – yet another indication of hatred and unreason dominating the world.

I've turned to Richard Crashaw, one of the lesser known poets of the century. His father was a strongly anti-papist vicar, and Crashaw was educated as an Anglican priest, but seems to have passed much of his life in uncertainty and despair. At the end of his life he found himself drawn to the Roman Catholic Church and spent his last years in Italy, though it's doubtful whether he actually converted. He had an especial devotion to Saint Teresa; his marvellous Hymn to Saint Teresa is too long to go here; but here's the shorter of two versions of another poem he wrote to her, *The Flaming Heart*, based on the iconography of the saint, in which she's always depicted with a seraphim plunging a flaming arrow into her heart. Like Bernini's famous statue of the saint, this poem also has a strong erotic charge.

### The Flaming Heart – Richard Crashaw

O heart, the equal poise of love's both parts,
Big alike with wounds and darts,
Live in these conquering leaves; live all the same,
And walk through all tongues one triumphant flame;
Live here, great heart, and love and die and kill,
And bleed and wound, and yield and conquer still.
Let this immortal life, where'er it comes,
Walk in a crowd of loves and martyrdoms;
Let mystic deaths wait on 't, and wise souls be
The love-slain witnesses of this life of thee.
O sweet incendiary! show here thy art,
Upon this carcass of a hard cold heart,

Let all thy scatter'd shafts of light, that play
Among the leaves of thy large books of day,
Combin'd against this breast, at once break in
And take away from me my self and sin;
This gracious robbery shall thy bounty be,
And my best fortunes such fair spoils of me.
O thou undaunted daughter of desires!
By all thy dow'r of lights and fires,
By all the eagle in thee, all the dove,
By all thy lives and deaths of love,
By thy large draughts of intellectual day,
And by thy thirsts of love more large than they,
By all thy brim-fill'd bowls of fierce desire,
By thy last morning's draught of liquid fire,
By the full kingdom of that final kiss
That seiz'd thy parting soul and seal'd thee his,
By all the heav'ns thou hast in him,
Fair sister of the seraphim!
By all of him we have in thee,
Leave nothing of my self in me:
Let me so read thy life that I
Unto all life of mine may die.

## June 20<sup>th</sup>

A drizzly grey day today, which reminded me of another, in Greece of all places, where we spent a holiday a few years ago. The other day, I read a moving article in the paper by somebody who'd set out on a journey to alleviate depression, taking with him an anthology of 'comfort' poems suggested by friends. This seemed to be a lovely thing to have; great poetry, read carefully, has the ability to comfort and console.

I first came across this poem, one of the greatest about the power of journeys, on that Greek holiday. We were visiting the great amphitheatre at Epidaurus. Our guide waited until were all sitting around on the huge circular sweep of benches, and then standing in the centre of the arena, read out this poem. The acoustics were perfect, and as she read it, everyone, all the other tourists in that great open space, fell silent and listened. It was mesmerising. And I cherish this poem as it was an especial favourite of our friend Belinda Hollyer.

**Ithaca – C.P. Cavafy (translated by George Valassopoulo)**
When you start on the way to Ithaca,
wish that the way be long,
full of adventure, full of knowledge.
The Laestrygones and the Cyclopes
and angry Poseidon, do not fear:
such on your way, you shall never meet
if your thoughts are lofty, if a noble
emotion touch your mind, your body.
The Laestrygones and the Cyclopes
and angry Poseidon you shall not meet
if you carry them not in your soul,
if your soul sets them not up before you.

Wish that the way be long,
that on many summer mornings,
with great pleasure, great delight,
you enter harbours for the first time seen;
that you stop at Phoenician marts,

and procure the goodly merchandise,
mother-of-pearl and corals, amber and ebony,
and sensual perfumes of all kinds,
plenty of sensual perfumes especially;
to wend your way to many Egyptian cities,
to learn and yet to learn from the wise.

Ever keep Ithaca in your mind,
your return thither is your goal.
But do not hasten at all your voyage,
better that it last for many years:
and full of years at length you anchor at your isle
rich with all that you gained on the way:
do not expect Ithaca to give you riches.

Ithaca gave you your fair voyage,
without her you would not have ventured on the way.
But she has no more to give you.

And if you find Ithaca a poor place,
she has not mocked you.
You have become so wise, so full of experience
that you should understand already what
these Ithacas mean.

## June 21st

Well, it was Midsummer Night last night, and we'd been promised a glorious moon, called a Strawberry Moon, a rare concurrence of full moon and solstice. After a bad start, the afternoon had been clear and bright, so we had hopes for a clear sky. But alas, as it grew dark, the sky was overcast and there was no moon to be seen. So I shall turn to an imaginary Midsummer night instead, and Oberon talking of poetic inspiration.

## From A Midsummer Night's Dream – William Shakespeare

The poet's eye, in a fine frenzy rolling,
Doth glance from heaven to earth, to earth from heaven;
And as imagination bodies forth
The forms of things unknown, the poet's pen
Turns them to shapes, and gives to airy nothing
A local habitation and a name.
Such tricks hath strong imagination
That, if it would but apprehend some joy,
It comprehends some bringer of that joy.
Or in the night, imagining some fear,
How easy is a bush supposed a bear.

## June 22nd

Tomorrow is the day when I fear the great British public will make a great British mistake, and vote to take us out of the EU – by Friday morning we shall know. Meanwhile, here's the poem that Richard suggested when I asked for comfort against despair poems – he thought that this lovely poem by Flecker would be a good accompaniment for any journey.

## The Golden Journey to Samarkand – James Elroy Flecker

We who with songs beguile your pilgrimage
And swear that Beauty lives though lilies die,
We Poets of the proud old lineage
Who sing to find your hearts, we know not why, -

What shall we tell you? Tales, marvellous tales
Of ships and stars and isles where good men rest,
Where nevermore the rose of sunset pales,
And winds and shadows fall towards the West:

And there the world's first huge white-bearded kings
In dim glades sleeping, murmur in their sleep,
And closer round their breasts the ivy clings,
Cutting its pathway slow and red and deep.

II
And how beguile you? Death has no repose
Warmer and deeper than the Orient sand
Which hides the beauty and bright faith of those
Who make the Golden Journey to Samarkand.

And now they wait and whiten peaceably,
Those conquerors, those poets, those so fair:
They know time comes, not only you and I,
But the whole world shall whiten, here or there;

When those long caravans that cross the plain
With dauntless feet and sound of silver bells
Put forth no more for glory or for gain,
Take no more solace from the palm-girt wells.

When the great markets by the sea shut fast
All that calm Sunday that goes on and on:
When even lovers find their peace at last,
And Earth is but a star, that once had shone.

## June 23rd

The worst has happened – a campaign of ignorance and scaremongering has won the day – Vladimir Putin and Marine Le Pen are our new best friends, and xenophobic vandalism has already hit our streets. Apart from anything else, I'm very sad; I liked being a European, and I'm absolutely sure that the system, though it had its faults, was best for our country. Now I feel mucky and ashamed of being British, and I don't like the feeling.

### A Last Word – Ernest Dowson

Let us go hence: the night is now at hand;
The day is overworn, the birds all flown;
And we have reaped the crops the gods have sown;
Despair and death; deep darkness o'er the land,
Broods like an owl; we cannot understand
Laughter or tears, for we have only known
Surpassing vanity: vain things alone
Have driven our perverse and aimless band.

Let us go hence, somewhither strange and cold,
To Hollow Lands where just men and unjust
Find end of labour, where's rest for the old,
Freedom to all from love and fear and lust.
Twine our torn hands! O pray the earth enfold
Our life-sick hearts and turn them into dust.

## June 28th

Nearly a week on from Cameron's ill-conceived referendum, and nothing gets any better. Our divided country is even more divided, Europe is shocked and angry, and our political parties are in disarray. Out of such muddles are ghastly political regimes born – all we can do now is hope that something good might come out of the mess. I remember John Betjeman being interviewed shortly before his death. He'd been a committed Christian but at the end of his life found his faith shaken in various ways. The interviewer asked him what he felt about religion now, as he approached the end; what was left to him. He thought about it for a long time, and answered quietly, 'Hope. Just hope.' With no faith and very little charity around at the moment, hope is all we have. A poem by George Herbert encourages us to keep hope alive in spite of difficulties.

**The Flower – George Herbert**
How fresh, oh Lord, how sweet and clean
Are thy returns! even as the flowers in spring:
   To which, beside their own demean,
The late-past frosts tributes of pleasure bring.
      Grief melts away
      Like snow in May
   As if there were no such cold thing.

   Who would have thought my shrivelled heart
Could have recovered greenness? It was gone
   Quite underground: as flowers depart
To see their mother-root, when they have blown,
      Where they together
      All the hard weather,
Dead to the world keep house unknown.

   These are thy wonders, Lord of power,
Killing and quickening, bringing down to hell

And up to heaven in an hour;
Making a chiming of a passing-bell.
    We say amiss
    This or that is:
They word is all, if we could spell.

Oh that I once past changing were,
Fast in thy Paradise, where no flower can wither!
    Many a spring I shoot up fair,
Offering at heaven, growing and groaning thither;
    Nor doth my flower
    Want a spring shower,
My sins and I joining together.

But while I grow in a straight line,
Still upwards bent, as if heaven were mine own,
    The anger comes, and I decline:
What frost to that? What pole is not the zone
    Where all things burn
    When thou dost turn,
And the least frown of thine is shown?

And now in age I bud again,
After so many deaths, I love and write;
    I once more smell the dew and rain,
And relish versing. Oh my only light,
    It cannot be
    That I am he
On whom thy tempests fell all night.

> These are thy wonders, Lord of love,
> To make us see we are but flowers that glide;
> Which when we once but find and prove,
> Thou hast a garden for us where to bide;
> Who would be more,
> Swelling through store,
> Forfeit their Paradise by their pride.

## June 29<sup>th</sup>

We'd planned a trip today, to cheer ourselves up – Wroxeter in the morning and lunch at Much Wenlock; all in a lovely setting of soft green Shropshire scenery. Much Wenlock, with its now ruined priory, might have turned into a city, but has remained a small market town. The priory was built on a site where the bones of St Milburga – who she? – were miraculously, or conveniently, rediscovered in the twelfth century. The website announces as one of the attractions 'heritage inspired shopping' – more teatowels, more marmalade, anyone? Its other claim to fame is that the Olympic Games were held there for the first time since classical days. We just like a pub that does excellent Ploughman's. Wroxeter is a short drive away – one of the few Roman cities which has been completely abandoned – the remains stand in the middle of a windy plain, with the Wrekin a blue smear in the distance. There isn't much to see now, except the ruins of the great basilica, which the locals called 'The Old Work' – it needs an act of imagination, but when you can apply this, it's an immensely evocative place, as you think of the ancient city, all blue woodsmoke and clattering cartwheels as far as the eye can see. Bits of Roman stuff are still to be seen in the old church, and no doubt all the local houses benefited too.

But alas, the rain is coming down so fast and so incessantly, so my journey to Wroxeter today must be an imaginary one, which is better than no journey at all, I guess. It was a visit to Wroxeter that inspired my book *Finding Minerva*, as I thought of a Wroxeter that had never been abandoned, and a Roman empire that had never collapsed. It's my favourite among my books, though, alas, not many people have read it.

Shropshire makes one think of Housman, though he wasn't really a Shropshire lad himself, he used its places and its memories. Uricon in this poem is Wroxeter (Viriconium.) Here's some bad border weather, very suited to the wind and rain that's battering us today.

### A Shropshire Lad XXXI – A. E. Housman

On Wenlock Edge the wood's in trouble;
    His forest fleece the Wrekin heaves;
The gale it piles the saplings double,
    And thick on Severn snow the leaves.

'Twould blow like this through holt and hanger,
    When Uricon the city stood:
'Tis the old wind in the old anger,
    But then it threshed another wood.

Then, 'twas before my time, the Roman
    At yonder heaving hill would stare:
The blood that warms and English yeoman,
    The thoughts that hurt him, they were there.

There, like the wind through woods in riot,
    Through him the gale of life blew high,

The tree of man was never quiet:
    Then 'twas the Roman, now 'tis I.

The gale, it plies the saplings double,
    It blows so hard, 'twill soon be gone:
Today the Roman and his trouble
    Are ashes under Uricon.

# *July*

## July 1st

I want to find something cheerful to look at for today, but it's the hundredth anniversary of the start of Battle of the Somme, and I can't ignore it. When I was a child, neither world war, first or second, meant very much to me. I was too young to have any memories of the second, and no-one close to my family was killed. My father was invalided out early on, and ended up with a safe, though boring job in Reading. My grandmother continually complained (she complained a lot) about shortages, as though it were somehow my fault, small boys were always drawing fighter planes, and there were black and white films in which clean-jawed heroes were terribly brave. My family had lost no-one close in World War One either – my father was then too young, and his family, living in a Rhondda mining valley, had reserved occupations. It all seemed very remote to me.

It wasn't until I was a teenager, and I read Robert Graves's *Goodbye to All That,* and the poems of Owen and Sassoon, that I started to understand what it had meant. I'd been taught to believe that God had a purpose in everything, but it was hard to see what purpose there could be in wiping out an entire generation of young men among such horrors of mud and blood.

Here's a quiet and thoughtful little poem written by Isaac Rosenberg, in his typical wry but passionate manner. An artist as well as a poet, he came from a poor Jewish East End family. He joined up in 1915, was sent to the Somme, and died in 1918. He was an unhappy soldier, ill-at-ease and not popular amongst his men. 'I never joined the army for patriotic reasons.' he said.

'Nothing can justify war. I suppose we must all fight to get the trouble over.'

## August 1914 – Isaac Rosenberg

What in our lives is burnt
In the fire of this?
The heart's dear granary?
The much we shall miss?

Three lives hath one life
Iron, honey, gold.
The gold gone, the honey gone –
Left is the hard and cold.

Iron are our lives
Molten right through our youth.
A burnt space through ripe fields
A fair mouth's broken tooth.

## July 6th

Still suffering from post-Brexit gloom, and with the Chilcot report due to come out later on today, I doubt that I'm going to feel cheered up, whatever its conclusions may be. Still, the sun is shining, which it hasn't been doing nearly enough this summer, and everything is washed in sparkling golden light. I've spent the morning going through old manuscripts – mostly the ones that never made it – a strange sensation. Some aren't up to the mark, but of others, turned down because…because of the many reasons publishers can find to make you feel bad … I think, well, this is okay; I'm still quite proud of this…

But today needs a poem, and not a gloomy one. And where better to go for a sense of calm wonder than Thomas Traherne, one of the few religious poets who can make religion seem desirable rather than terrifying. His description of the innocence and glory of childhood prefigures Wordsworth and Blake; his sense of the beauties of the world balances out the usual seventeenth-century view of the world as a place of sin and gloom. Even jewels and laces, those manifestations of sinful vanity, excite his sense of beauty and awe.

**Wonder – Thomas Traherne**
How like an angel I came down!
    How bright are all things here!
When first among his works I did appear
    O how their Glory did me crown!
The world resembled His Eternity,
    In which my soul did walk;
And every thing that I did see
    Did with me talk.

The skies in their magnificence,
    The lively, lovely air;
Oh how divine, how soft, how sweet, how fair!
    The stars did entertain my sense,
And all the works of God, so bright and pure,
    So rich and great did seem,
As if they ever must endure
    In my esteem.

A native health and innocence
    Within my bones did grow,

And while my God did all his Glories show,
    I felt a vigour in my sense
That was all Spirit. I within did flow
    With seas of life, like wine;
I nothing in the world did know
    But 'twas divine.

Harsh ragged objects were concealed,
    Oppressions, tears and cries,
Sins, griefs, complaints, dissensions, weeping eyes
Were hid, and only things revealed
Which heavenly Spirits and the Angels prize.
    The state of Innocence,
And bliss, not trades and poverties,
    Did fill my sense.

The streets were paved with golden stones,
    The boys and girls were mine,
Oh how did all their lovely faces shine!
The sons of men were holy ones,
In joy and beauty they appeared to me,
    And every thing which here I found,
While like an angel I did see,
    Adorned the ground.

Rich diamond and pearl and gold
    In every place was seen,
Rare splendours, yellow, blue, red, white and green,
    Mine eyes did everywhere behold.
Great wonders clothed with glory did appear,
    Amazement was my bliss,

That and my wealth was everywhere;
> No joy to this!

Cursed and devised proprieties,
> With envy, avarice
And fraud, those fiends that spoil even Paradise,
> Flew from the splendour of mine eyes,
And so did hedges, limits, bounds,
> I dreamed not aught of those,
But wandered over all men's grounds,
> And found repose.

Proprieties themselves were mine
> And hedges ornaments,
Walls, boxes, coffers, and their rich contents
> Did not divide my joys, but all combine.
Clothes, ribbons, jewels,laces, I esteemed
> My joys by others worn:
For me they all to wear them seemed
> When I was born.

## July 9th

We're bad at remembering our wedding anniversary, and usually let the day slip past unnoticed. Still, we managed to remember last year's which was our fiftieth, and had a celebration with the family in a restaurant in St Katharine Docks on a beautiful sunny day. It was a day I shall remember with more pleasure than our actual wedding, which was a gloomy occasion all round. I never wanted a big fancy wedding, so the quiet registry office do was fine by me, but religion managed to raise its nasty head and take away any pleasantness there might have been. My mother was upset because I wouldn't marry in a Catholic church, but the religion was an unflinching one which meant you couldn't marry without taking the sacrament, making your partner go through a course of instruction, and promising to bring your children up as Catholics, and I couldn't see any way around this with my burgeoning agnosticism. All the local priests of course joined forces to make me feel really bad. Even my atheist father didn't support me, suggesting I should just 'go along with it'. I was sorry to upset my mother, but felt I had no choice. And on the other side of the religious fence, Richard's nasty step-father disliked me because I wasn't Jewish, and he decided to spend our wedding day being ill. After our quiet service at Kensington Registry Office, our witness, Richard's best friend, went home, and we trooped back to my mother-in-law's flat for smoked salmon sandwiches, keeping our voices down because of the invalid in his sickroom, who didn't offer us a good wish or a smile. My mother was morose, my father had too much to drink, no-one thought of taking a photograph. In the afternoon, we went quietly back to our little flat in Bloomsbury, breathing sighs of relief. It was a day I was glad to escape from. So the fiftieth anniversary had something of a triumph about it – we were still here, still together and had acquired a lovely family to be enthusiastic and supportive of us. Everyone was happy, we laughed, ate well, blew out candles and exchanged presents. The sun shone, the sky was turquoise blue and we looked out at beautiful expensive yachts stirring gently in the water. So there, I thought. And we came back to Wales to find a lovely bouquet from our neighbours in the village. This year, our fifty-first wasn't nearly such an event, but it's always good to find yourself still alive on these occasions, so we went out to a favourite local restaurant and had champagne and lobster. So there, again.

Here's a strange, rather dour little poem by Hardy, about a long married couple and their feelings for each other. Hardy seemed to prefer his wives dead rather than alive, but it's a thoughtful poem, in spite of its melancholy mood. Being long-married can do strange things to you; quite often Richard and I come out with the same words at once as we try to describe something, or find we have the same thought simultaneously. We know when the other is bored or made cross by an occasion, even if we're good at keeping the expression out of our faces. We know what will please, what will annoy. Fifty years is a very long time, and certainly 'life's flushest feather' has long faded, but there are consolations to be had from the lack of brightness.

## Between Us Now – Thomas Hardy

Between us now and here –
    Two thrown together
Who are not wont to wear
    Life's flushest feather-
Who see the scenes slide past,
The daytimes dimming past,
Let there be truth at last,
    Even if despair.

So thoroughly and long
    Have you now known me,
So real in faith and strong
    Have I now shown me,
That nothing needs disguise
Further in any wise,
Or asks or justifies
    A guarded tongue.

Face unto face, then, say
    Eyes my own meeting,
Is your heart far away,
    Or with mine beating?
When false things are brought low,
And swift things have grown slow,
Feigning like froth shall go,
Faith be for aye.

## July 13th

It's late evening, and the light is starting to stiffen and flatten like a stage set. Everything has gone very still and quiet. And then suddenly a last wash of sun paints the hill an astonishing daffodil yellow, such as I've never seen before. It soon fades, of course, as astonishing light does, and an hour or so later, we have a sunset. Because of the poor weather we've been getting, it's the first we've had for ages. Yes, there are streaks of rose pink, and apricot, and I can see them clearly with my newly operated-on eye. So I'm not going to miss sunsets after all. I shall celebrate this in conceited fashion by posting one I made earlier – a poem I wrote some time ago, for Richard's choir – the only thing I've ever written that's been set to music; by the organist and composer Meirion Wynn Jones. It's a strange and flattering thing to hear your writing taken over by music – seeing how music can heighten dull lines and add new meaning to others. I especially remember how the 'hazy clouds of insects' sounded – just like hazy clouds of insects, in fact.

**Evening**
Red light stains the hill;
Crows come wheeling, crying,
All their black battalions
Coming home

Swallows on the phone wires,
Sitting there like music;
Hazy clouds of insects
Hover round.

Hiding in the branches,
Ruffling her feathers,
Owl waits unblinking,
Looking down

Shadows crowd together
Marshalling their forces,
Sun slides down the valley,
Sinking fast.

The watcher at the bridge
Lingering no longer
Shouldering his rucksack,
Going home.

**July 15th**
A year that started off dark has turned darker still with the atrocity in Nice, following on from the earlier atrocities in Turkey and Iraq. It's hard to believe, as the cliché would have it, that love conquers

all and good will triumph in the end; it seems at the moment that evil must always come out on top because it can. No matter how much love was generated at the funeral of Jo Cox, she can never come back to her children or to the refugees she was helping. Her murderer has won. As has the deranged lorry driver in Nice; one man and the action of a moment can leave hundreds of lives shattered. And to what end?

And yet all we can do in the face of it is to stay true to our own sense of what is right and loving – very few of us can be good, but we can all be kind, and if enough of us are, then maybe one day, it will seep through into the consciences of those deluded and ruined young men.

Here's a sonnet from someone who's hit rock bottom and sees no consolation. In 1885-6 Gerard Manley Hopkins wrote a sequence of poems known as his *Terrible Sonnets,* which he never published during his lifetime, but left to be found after his death. No despair can be imagined deeper than this – nothing, not even his religion, can offer any comfort. The mountains of the mind have seldom been more painfully examined. A sonnet that suits a day without hope.

## Gerard Manley Hopkins Sonnet 41

No worst, there is none. Pitched past pitch of grief,
More pangs will, schooled at forepangs, wilder wring.
Comforter, where, where is your comforting?
Mary, mother of us, where is your relief?
My cries heave, herds-long; huddle in a main, a chief
Woe, world-sorrow; on an age-old anvil wince and sing—
Then lull, then leave off. Fury had shrieked 'No ling-
ering! Let me be fell: force I must be brief'.

O the mind, mind has mountains; cliffs of fall
Frightful, sheer, no-man-fathomed. Hold them cheap
May who ne'er hung there. Nor does long our small
Durance deal with that steep or deep. Here! creep,
Wretch, under a comfort serves in a whirlwind: all
Life death does end and each day dies with sleep.

## July 18<sup>th</sup>

After all this despair, I turn again to the seventeenth century, and the calm faith of its poets. I remember a couple of years ago we went on a Henry Vaughan walk, ('clearly waymarked') or at least we tried to, but of course missed at the first turning, so we went on a non-Henry Vaughan walk along a canal which he wouldn't have known. But so what – it was a beautiful spring day, celandines, lady's smock, drowsy bumblebees, a Red Admiral, a heron, and the deep red Brecon soil. No wonder he wrote poetry in this valley, still tranquil now in spite of the noisy A40 which hurtles mercilessly through it. We did find his grave, though, beneath an ancient yew, in a dark corner of the steep churchyard of Llansaintfraidd which almost tumbles down to the road. *At his request,* said the inscription, if my Latin is good enough, *these words were inscribed; Ineffectual servant, great sinner, here I lie...* I was sad I hadn't brought a few daffodils to lay on the dark mossy slab.

During the Civil War, he was exiled from here. His twin brother, the alchemist, left the area and died in Oxford. Maybe Henry's last years weren't so peaceful after all. But his legacy is the poems and their deep tranquillity. Also his love for the countryside around here, as demonstrated by this poem. It's interesting to see the word 'country' used, as we use it now, to mean the countryside as opposed to the town.

## Retirement – Henry Vaughan

Fresh fields and woods! the Earth's fair face,
God's foot-stool, and man's dwelling-place.
I ask not why the first Believer
Did love to be a country liver?
Who to secure pious content
Did pitch by groves and wells his tent;
Where he might view the boundless sky,
And all those glorious lights on high;
With flying meteors, mists and show'rs,
Subjected hills, trees, meads and flow'rs;
And ev'ry minute bless the King
And wise Creator of each thing.
I ask not why he did remove
To happy Mamre's holy grove,
Leaving the cities of the plain
To Lot and his successless train?
All various lusts in cities still
Are found; they are the thrones of ill;
The dismal sinks, where blood is spill'd,
Cages with much uncleanness fill'd.
But rural shades are the sweet fense
Of piety and innocence.
They are the Meek's calm region, where
Angels descend and rule the sphere,
Where heaven lies leiger, and the dove
Duly as dew, comes from above.
If Eden be on Earth at all,
'Tis that, which we the country call.

## July 21st

One of the few advantages of our all-too-frequent hospital journeys is the journey through the beautiful Herefordshire countryside, all soft fields and orchards, the verges lush with the wild flowers of mid-summer, willowherb, meadowsweet and cow parsley. Herefordshire also probably has the best soft fruit in the world, and we come home with our car bursting with punnets of ripe strawberries, raspberries, ridiculously plump cherries, velvety plums and jewellike currants. So what better poem for today than Christina Rossetti's Goblin Market, where the poet manages to override her inner censor sufficiently to tell this strange story of temptation and redemption through love. Few have managed to write so sensuously of fruits and flavours, especially as the fruit has the added frisson of being forbidden.

### *From* Goblin Market – Christina Rossetti

Morning and evening
Maids heard the goblins cry
'Come buy our orchard fruits,
Come buy, come buy.
Apples and quinces,
Dates and sharp bullaces,
Lemons and oranges,
Plump unpecked cherries,
Melons and raspberries,
Bloom-down-cheeked peaches,
Swart headed mulberries,
Wild free-born cranberries,
Crab-apples, dewberries,
Pine-apples, blackberries,
Apricots, strawberries,

All ripe together
In summer weather —
Morns that pass by,
Fair eves that fly;
Come buy come buy,
Our grapes fresh from the vine,
Pomegranates full and fine,
Rare pears and greengages,
Damsons and bilberries,
Taste them and try,
Currants and goosberries,
Bright fire-like barberries,
Figs to fill your mouth,
Citrons from the south,
Sweet to tongue and sound to eye,
Come buy, come buy.'
Evening by evening,
Among the brookside rushes,
Laura bowed her head to hear,
Lizzie veiled her blushes,
Crouching close togeter,
In the cooling weather,
With clasping arms and cautioning lips,
With tingling cheeks and finger tips.
'Lie close,' Laura said,
Pricking up her golden head:
'We must not look at goblin men,
We must not buy their fruits.
Who knows upon what soil they feed
Their hungry thirsty roots?'

## July 26th

Barely a day seems to go by now without some young man trying to kill lots of people in the name of something or other. Today's gift to a grateful Allah was the murder of an eighty-four year old priest, who had his throat cut in front of his altar.

And the day of Trump seems to be getting nearer – trying to imagine the World Belonging To Trump, and it's not a nice place. Maybe the reality will be better than the fear, but I don't think so. Oh how we're going to miss the civilised and gracious Obamas.

So a time of quiet contemplation – the only way to escape from the horrors of real life. And who better to turn to than Sir Philip Sidney, poet, courtier, soldier, hero, the golden boy of the sixteenth century, whose sonnets to Stella are among the most beautiful of his age. I love the calm, slow pace of this poem, its mood of tranquillity, its slow rhythm that echoes a gentle saunter beneath trees. And how brave to use a five-syllable word as the keynote of the poem. It's been beautifully set to music by Dowland.

### *From* Solitariness – Sir Philip Sidney

O sweet woods, the delight of solitariness!
Oh, how much I do like your solitariness!
Where man's mind hath a freed consideration,
Of goodness to receive lovely direction.
Where senses do behold th' order of heav'nly host,
And wise thoughts do behold what the creator is;
Contemplation here holdeth his only seat,
Bounded with no limits, born with a wing of hope,
Climbs even unto the stars, nature is under it.
Nought disturbs thy quiet, all to thy service yields,
Each sight draws on a thought (thought, mother of science)
Sweet birds kindly do grant harmony unto thee,

Fair trees' shade is enough fortification,
Nor danger to thyself if 't be not in thyself.

# August

## August 3rd

A friend tells me that it's the birthday of Ernest Dowson, that young and very *fin de siècle* poet of the nineteenth century. His life, marked by alchoholism, depression, and that propensity many Victorian men had for falling in love with young girls, seems to typify decadence, but he was a clever scholar. He was friends with Wilde and Beardsley, and ended his short life – he was thirty-two when he died – a Catholic. This is probably his most famous poem.

## They are not long – Ernest Dowson
*Vitae summa brevis spem nos vetat incohare longam.*

They are not long, the weeping and the laughter,
Love and desire and hate;
I think they have no portion in us after
We pass the gate.

They are not long, the days of wine and roses,
Out of a misty dream
Our path emerges for a while, then closes
Within a dream.

## August 11th

The Perseid meteor shower is supposed to be at its best tonight, and it's predicted to be a beautiful showing of them. Three nights ago when I looked out of the window at 2 am, the sky was ablaze with stars, but there were no meteors to be seen. Then the next night and the next, the sky was overcast. I think it's going to be overcast tonight; the sky is dingy grey and thick, though the sun is struggling to break through, so my meteor shower tonight is going to be an imaginary one, and this suits Housman and his habitual faint note of melancholy and loss. He seems to be writing of a kind of impersonal, even cold, eternal progression in nature, as, in some of his other poems, he mourns his lost love; an inevitable loss, since in those days a forbidden one.

I think of him spending the last years of his life in a rather pleasant Highgate street – I don't think he would have seen many stars from his window there, however.

### *From* More Poems no VII – A.E. Housman

Stars, I have seen them fall,
    But when they drop and die
No star is lost at all
    From all the star-sown sky.
The toil of all that be
    Helps not the primal fault;
It rains into the sea,
    And still the sea is salt.

## August 14th

Another poem from William Soutar chosen by Jane. I like it for its calmness and dignity, and the sense that even in the darkest times, there's a glimmer of light.

### In the Time of Tyrants – William Soutar

All that the hand may touch;
All that the hand may own;
Crumbles beyond time's clutch
Down to oblivion.

Fear not the boasts which wound:
Fear not the threats which bind:
Always on broken ground
The seeds fall from the mind.

Always in darkest loam
A birthday is begun;
And from its catacomb
A candle lights the sun.

## August 16th

Poetry is a strange beast. I must have come across this poem years ago in a childhood anthology, saw it again briefly a few years ago, then forgot about it. But then yesterday, for no apparent reason it popped into my head and started jumping about noisily there, making itself heard. I don't know what brought it back – I don't think I've ever slept on an island; I'm not one of life's happy campers. But somehow this poem leaves the experience in your head.

I don't know anything about the writer, except that she was an American who wrote many books and poems mainly for children.

### If once you have slept on an island – Rachel Field

If once you have slept on an island
You'll never be quite the same;
You may look as you looked the day before
And go by the same old name,
You may bustle about in street and shop
You may sit at home and sew,

But you'll see blue water and wheeling gulls
Wherever your feet may go.

You may chat with the neighbors of this and that
And close to your fire keep,
But you'll hear ship whistle and lighthouse bell
And tides beat through your sleep.
Oh! you won't know why and you can't say how
Such a change upon you came,
But once you have slept on an island,
You'll never be quite the same.

## August 18th

Our friend Colin Tucker sends me this poem. He says that it's probably his favourite love poem. It is very beautiful, and shows how sensitive Burns can be, and how unusual to find someone writing about love in old age.

## John Anderson, my jo, John – Robert Burns

> John Anderson, my jo, John,
> When we were first acquent;
> Your locks were like the raven,
> Your bonnie brow was brent;
> But now your brow is beld, John,
> Your locks are like the snaw;
> But blessings on your frosty pow,
> John Anderson, my jo.
>
> John Anderson, my jo, John,
> We clamb the hill thegither;

And mony a cantie day, John,
We've had wi' ane anither:
Now we maun totter down, John,
And hand in hand we'll go,
And sleep thegither at the foot,
John Anderson, my jo.

## August 22$^{nd}$

We're spending a week in Pembrokeshire by the sea, partly because it's beautiful, and partly so that the grandchildren can have an old-fashioned seaside holiday. However sophisticated they are with their mastery of laptops and iphones, the lure of buckets and spades and paddling in the lacy edges of foam still draws them in. Richard seems to think it's extremely laughable that I enjoyed this as a child; I'm not quite sure why – maybe he classes it as one of my funny working class habits like putting vinegar on my chips. His holidays, with his wicked stepfather, were sophisticated and dull. Holidays for us were simply going to stay with a family member. Until I was about five, I had an aunt who lived by the seaside, and I used to visit with my grandmother, although it was her habit to make every experience into a punishment. One day, I remember I was seized with an urge to go further and further out into the clear blue water; I went on and on, seeing the edge of the enclosing bay getting nearer, leaving most of the paddlers behind, and feeling the water coming up to my thighs. I had no sense of danger and no intention of turning back – perhaps I thought I would metamorphose into a mermaid and be swept away to palaces of coral and pearls. I don't think I was very far out, though, when I was aware of people shouting at me, and I turned to see my frantic grandmother, dressed in hat and coat, waving furiously at me. It might have been that occasion, or another, when she told me I'd been so naughty that she was never ever going to take me to the seaside again. And she never did. What she knew then, and I didn't, was that my aunt and uncle were about to move inland anyway so the opportunity wouldn't have arisen, but she preferred to convey the information as unkindly as possible.

I like this little poem by Robert Louis Stevenson, which sticks in my mind whenever I think of the sea. His invalid childhood made him especially sensitive and responsive to impressions, and in these little poems, unlike most poems written for children which tend to have a didactic air, he simply immerses himself in the mindset of a child, and experiences a simple but magical pleasure – in this case, the delight in being given a spade, and the mystery of the sea endlessly filling up the holes he digs.

## When I was down beside the sea – Robert Louis Stevenson

When I was down beside the sea
A wooden spade they gave to me
To dig the sandy shore.

My holes were empty like a cup.
In every hole the sea came up,
Till it could come no more.

## August 23rd

Waking up in the morning in our rented Pembrokeshire cottage, we look over low fields with their roughened surfaces, caught in an uneven netting of tumbled stone walls and stunted gorse hedges. There are unbelievable sunsets, streaked and marbled golden-pink. In the hedgerows, wildflowers grow in prolific pre-industrial masses, red and white campion, toadflax, purple vetch, corn cockle, scabious, thrift. There are brown butterflies everywhere, like old ladies' frilly silk dresses. We've had very few butterflies in our garden this year, so it's lovely to see them in such profusion. They are all over the land, but also fly around the sea, which inspired me to this little poem.

I've also been looking up the names for butterflies in various languages – many of them are almost little poems in themselves: *mariposa* (Spanish); *farfalle* (Italian); *Schmetterlinge* (German); *papillon* (French); *paru paro* (Filipino); *sommerfugl* (Norwegian); *bolboreta* (Galician); *pili pala* (Welsh); *petalonda* (Greek); *babochka* (Russian). Presumably the word for 'slug' or 'worm' isn't beautiful in any language.

**Butterflies at sea.**
There are butterflies by the sea,
Small brown scraps of silk,
Dancing and hovering over the sand.

Gulls, in their element, scream and plunge,
The cold salt air is theirs,
No need for honey and sunshine
In their icy world

But these various butterflies
Inspecting the sand and stones;
Something is keeping them here. What?

Soon they'll die; you'd think they'd go amongst flowers,
Nectar, bright colours, soft airs.
There's no accounting for taste.

## August 24th

We go with the family to Castell Henllys, the reconstituted Iron Age fort; not far away is the house where my grandfather was born and where all the Thomases came from. One of the good things about having Welsh blood is that, thanks to family bibles and family stories, you know an awful lot about ancestors. I can trace the Thomases back to the eighteenth century; the eighteenth-century David Thomas, my great-great grandfather, was a builder, and helped to build the rather fine Baptist chapel, Bethabara, at Pontyglasier. Among the nineteenth-century Thomases were Baptist ministers and several poets who wrote in strict Welsh metre. I imagine them all, dressed solemnly, black-hatted, lined up and staring at me rather disapprovingly. *Duw duw, is this what the family has come to now?*

As we visit the hill fort, it's a spooky thought that quite possibly, since people tended to be static in the past, my own ancestors might well be among those shadowy Iron Age inhabitants of the place, and my DNA in their bones.

Children's activities had been laid on at the hill fort when we arrived, since it was the school holidays, and for small children, there isn't a lot to enjoy in a reconstituted hut. There was the usual array of face painting, fighting, story telling. Jacob made a good little Iron Age fighter, and Lily charmed us all by proving to have extremely good slingshot skills, far better than all the other children, including the usual competitive older boys, who were lining up restlessly, panting to have a go. Lily just stood there calmly, aimed, and hit the target nearly every time. True, her weapons were lumps of bread dough, and the wild boars she hit were painted, but if we were relying on her for our Iron Age breakfast, we wouldn't go hungry; Lily the Slingshot Queen.

Here's Hardy, writing about the traces of the distant past in the present day landscape, and how his own memories link to those traces. He's thinking of the Romans and I'm not sure the Romans ever got as far as Ceredigion, but our part of Powys is crisscrossed with Roman roads and camps and forts.

**The Roman Road – Thomas Hardy**
The Roman Road runs straight and bare
As the pale parting-line in hair
Across the heath. And thoughtful men
Contrast its days of Now and Then,
And delve, and measure and compare;
Visioning on the vacant air
Helmed legionaries, who proudly rear
The Eagle, as they pace again
The Roman Road.
But no tall brass-helmed legionnaire
Haunts it for me. Uprises there
A mother's form upon my ken,
Guiding my infant steps, as when
We walked that ancient thoroughfare,
The Roman Road.

# *September*

## September 5th

In London, the anniversary of the Great Fire of 1666, we arrive in time to see the spectacle of a stunning wooden model of the seventeenth-century skyline about to be set on fire over the river Thames (though in cowardly fashion, we watch it only on the television). Dreadful to have seen one's city, which had seemed so permanent, reduced to ashes, and to lose a lifetime of accumulated possessions. I was too young to remember the second great fire of London in wartime, but I recall the bomb sites everywhere, scattered with rubble, with clouds of willowherb and sprouting buddleia. And the strange appearance of destroyed houses, a fireplace stuck halfway up a wall, and scraps of fancy wallpaper waving in the breeze; you wondered about the people whose familiar homes they were, the night that fire and death rained down from the skies. It's been suggested that one of the factors that drove Virginia Woolf to suicide was seeing the destruction of her beloved city; a city that appears almost as a character in her book. Houses, shops, churches, alleyways and great streets, all gone for ever.

Some believed that after the Great Fire, London had a chance to rise again, not as a crowded and insanitary jumble of streets, but as a glorious Jerusalem, and it's this prospect that Dryden tries out in this poem. But of course this never happened; human nature, in all its imperfections, prevailed, and the new London was pretty much as crowded and messy as the old. Apart of course, from Wren's St Paul's, which we'd never have had without the destruction.

## After the Great Fire of London – John Dryden

Methinks already from this chymic flame
I see a city of more precious mould,
Rich as the town which gives the Indies name,
With silver paved and all divine with gold.

Already, labouring with a mighty fate,
She shakes the rubbish from her mounting brow,
And seems to have renewed her charter's date,
Which Heaven will to the death of time allow.

More great than human now and more august,
New deified she from her fires does rise:
Hew widening streets on new foundations trust,
And, opening, into larger parts she flies.

Before, she like some shepherdess did show
Who sat to bathe her by a river's side,
Not answering to her fame, but rude and low,
Nor taught the beauteous arts of modern pride.

Now like a maiden queen she will behold
From her high turrets hourly suitors come;
The East with incense and the West with gold
Will stand like suppliants to receive her doom.

The silver Thames, her own domestic flood,
Shall bear her vessels like a sweeping train,
And often wind, as of his mistress proud,
With longing eyes to meet her face again.

The wealthy Tagus and the wealthier Rhine
The glory of their towns no more shall boast,
And Seine, that would with Belgian rivers join,
Shall find her lustre stained and traffic lost.

The venturous merchant who designed more far
And touches on our hospitable shore,
Charmed with the splendour of this northern star,
Shall here unlade him and depart no more.

## September 12th

Yesterday we went to an apple celebration at the house of friends, lovely orchards with trees laden with fruit; and it inspired us to go and look at our own neglected orchard. The apples were small, and not quite ripe, but the colours were lovely, crimson, scarlet, russet and green. Most will fall into the grass, though I'm inspired to make an apple cake today.

The poem running through my head is this masterpiece by Keats; one of those poems that we've all read in youth but probably not much since. We had to 'do' Keats at A-level, which rather spoiled him for me for many years, but the words remained in my head and come back to please me now. Such lines as *To bend with apples the mossed cottage trees*, Or *sinking as the light wind lives or dies*, the sudden beautiful personification of Autumn in the second verse *hair soft lifted by the winnowing wind*, or keeping her *laden head steady across a brook* are quite magical, and you just want to fit them in your mouth and keep saying them over and over.

## Ode To Autumn – John Keats

Season of mists and mellow fruitfulness,
Close bosom-friend of the maturing sun;
Conspiring with him how to load and bless
With fruit the vines that round the thatch-eaves run;
To bend with apples the mossed cottage-trees,
And fill all fruit with ripeness to the core;
To swell the gourd, and plump the hazel shells
With a sweet kernel; to set budding more,
And still more, later flowers for the bees,
Until they think warm days will never cease,
For Summer has o'er-brimmed their clammy cells.

Who hath not seen thee oft amid thy store?
Sometimes whoever seeks abroad may find
Thee sitting careless on a granary floor,
Thy hair soft-lifted by the winnowing wind;
Or on a half-reaped furrow sound asleep,
Drowsed with the fume of poppies, while thy hook
Spares the next swath and all its twined flowers;
And sometimes like a gleaner thou dost keep
Steady thy laden head across a brook;
Or by a cider-press, with patient look,
Thou watchest the last oozings, hours by hours.

Where are the songs of Spring? Ay, where are they?
Think not of them, thou hast thy music too,
While barred clouds bloom the soft-dying day,
And touch the stubble-plains with rosy hue;
Then in a wailful choir, the small gnats mourn
Among the river sallows, borne aloft

Or sinking as the light wind lives or dies;
And full-grown lambs loud bleat from hilly bourn;
Hedge-crickets sing; and now with treble soft
The redbreast whistles from a garden-croft,
And gathering swallows twitter in the skies.

## September 21$^{st}$

Autumn continues, golden days alternating with drab. But when the sun is shining on amber leaves and the hills are impossibly green-and-gold, there can be no better season. And fruit is in abundance – our bright Discovery apples, with crimson skins and red stained creamy flesh, drop heavily into the grass. A friend brings us a bag of damsons, which I make into glorious rich purple jam – I've never been much of a jam maker, but this year there seems to be so much of everything that I've got no choice. Rowan trees are hung with heavy clusters of berries, and scarlet branches hang from the hawthorn trees like red waterfalls. Late convolvulous winds exuberantly over the hedges, and our rugosa rose has huge orange hips.

Here's that always surprising Welsh poet W.H. Davies writing about these lush days.

## Rich Days – W. H. Davies

Welcome to you, rich Autumn days,
Ere comes the cold, leaf-picking wind;
When golden stocks are seen in fields,
All standing arm-in-arm entwined;
And gallons of sweet cider seen
On trees in apples red and green.
With mellow pears that cheat our teeth,
Which melt that tongues may suck them in,

With blue-black damsons, yellow plums,
And woodnuts rich, to make us go
Into the loneliest lanes we know.

## September 25th

*Apple* is also one of those words that is evocative in many languages. *Apple*, *apfel* and *afal* all give the sense of biting into the crisp fruit. *Pomme* sits heavy and fragrant in the hand, *mela* tastes of honey. John Drinkwater's poem *Moonlit Apples* is one of the most beautiful about this beautiful fruit. It feels like a painting by Eric Ravilious with the diagonal shafts of moonlight, and the pale crystalline colours.

### Moonlit Apples – John Drinkwater

At the top of the house the apples are laid in rows,
And the skylight lets the moonlight in, and those
Apples are deep-sea apples of green. There goes
A cloud on the moon in the autumn night.

A mouse in the wainscot scratches, and scratches, and then
There is no sound at the top of the house of men
Or mice; and the cloud is blown and the moon again
Dapples the apples with deep-sea light.
They are lying in rows there, under the gloomy beams;
On the sagging floor, they gather the silver streams
Out of the moon, those moonlit apples of dreams,
And quiet is the steep stair under.

In the corridors under there is nothing but sleep.
And stiller than ever on orchard boughs they keep
Tryst with the moon, and deep is the silence, deep
On moon-washed apples of wonder.

## September 28th

We're spending a couple of days in Paris on our way to Spain; we walk in the Luxembourg Gardens in bright autumn sunlight, and go to the Musee D'Orsay where we haven't been for many years. It's a sprawling confusing gallery, with gems buried among acres of dull academic works. But among the gems are some Van Gogh paintings, a marvellous self portait, in which the artist looks out painfully alert, from a soft blue background, one of the starry sky paintings, and the last of three paintings he made of his bedroom in Arles. I'm annoyed at the starry sky painting – hordes of people stand in front of it, making it hard for me to see, and NOT ONE OF THEM IS LOOKING AT IT. Instead they are holding up their phones to do the looking instead. Are we raising a generation of people who have forgotten how to use their eyes?

But almost no-one stands in front of the bedroom picture, and we're able to look long at it. When Van Gogh writes to his brother Theo the words he uses about his colours are almost like a poem in themselves, the subtle gradation of shades, the way they interact and contrast, butter-yellow and lemon-green, pale violet and lilac, and the emotional meanings he invests in them.

## *From* The Letters of Vincent Van Gogh – Letter to Theo, Arles, October 1898

...This time it's just simply my bedroom, only here colour is to do everything, and giving by its simplification a grander style to things is to be suggestive here of *rest* or of sleep in general. In a word, to look at the picture ought to rest the brain, or rather the imagination.

The walls are pale violet. The floor is of red tiles.

The wood of the bed and chairs is the yellow of fresh butter, the sheets and pillows very light lemon-green.

The coverlet scarlet. The window green.

The toilet table orange, the basin blue.

The doors lilac.

That is all – there is nothing in this room with closed shutters. The broad lines of the furniture must again express inviolable rest. Portraits on the walls, and a mirror and a towel and some clothes.

The frame – as there is no white in the picture – will be white.

# *October*

**October 5th**

Just back from a lovely six days in Spain, a country we still don't know well enough, and wanted to fill in some gaps. Apart from the drama of falling down the stairs in a lurching TGV and ending up covered in blood, everything went well. Though we spent our first Barcelona evening in A&E, where I was slotted into the system, a foreigner just off the street, without fuss, and though there was a bit of a wait, was seen by a very sweet doctor, given a very reassuring x-ray – my bones are dodgy but nothing was broken – had staples put in my head wound – and was sent out really none the worse for wear. Oh, how sad that we're not going to be European any more.

We saw the Sagrada Familia Cathedral (technically a basilica, not a cathedral) with coloured light pouring through the stained glass windows – quite magical, quite mad. Then we went on to Madrid, really for the sole purpose of seeing the Prado (bit of a bucket list, this holiday) and Las Meninas. The Prado was well worth it, although Durer's stunning self-portrait was out on loan, and The Garden Of Earthly Delights was obscured by a horde of people with audioguides not letting anyone near it. Actually I was quite glad, because, though it's uncool to say so, I don't like Bosch. And the Goyas were magnificent.

But Las Meninas lived up to all expectation. The first thing you notice as you go into the long gallery where it's hung is how luminous it is. Light from those tall windows laps around the feet of the main personages, warming the darkness of the whole composition; a contrast to the flat brightness of the other Habsburg court portraits. This luminosity doesn't show at all in reproduction, so the train journey to Madrid was worth it. We'd also been lucky enough in Barcelona to see Picasso's riffs on the painting, grotesque and strange as were many of the pictures, they brought out hidden meanings, the surrounding play of hands – there are many hands in the painting – and the stare, especially of the dwarf woman; sometimes hostile, sometimes amused, sometimes enigmatic.

The little blonde princess, Margareta Theresa, went on, in true Habsburg fashion, to marry her uncle, Leopold I of Austria, who was 'of a weak and sickly consitution, ordinary in countenance, and distinguished with an unusual portion of the Austrian lip.' Among a mass of other titles, she became the Holy Roman Empress. She was married for six years, had four children and some miscarriages. Only one of her children survived to adulthood. But Margareta and her unprepossesing husband were happy, apparently, until she died in childbirth at twenty-one; he mourned her for the rest of his life. But you needn't feel too sorry for her; she was rabidly anti-semitic, and caused the Jews to be expelled from Vienna on the grounds that she thought they'd been responsible for the deaths of her children.

I wrote a poem about Las Meninas, since I could find no other way of expressing what I saw in it, and what stood out for me afterwards.

**Las Meninas**
I'm looking at you.
That's why he put me at the front, to look at you.
Though you don't want to look at me,
Only at my mistress with the silver-spun hair and priceless dress;
Caught in a net of hands, she wants for nothing,
Except perhaps to run barefoot in the grass.

What does *he* think, in his dark corner?
Only his art will say, and his art will say only what he wants.
Do you see a ghost king? And a queen?
Do they even think at all?

And he, bisecting the bright doorway
Will he turn his back on us?
You wouldn't blame him

Can you see me now?
Ah, you see me now.
But you don't know what *I'm* thinking;
You'll never know.

## October 6th

It's National Poetry Day today, though I'm not quite sure what that means. Still, a good excuse to post one of those poems I loved as a teenager, though I find it a bit overblown now in my austere old age. Still, it's very passionate, very intense, and encapsulates the powerful imagination of the young.

### Romance – W. J. Turner

When I was but thirteen or so
    I went into a golden land,
Chimborazo, Cotopaxi
    Took me by the hand.

My father died, my brother too,
    They passed like fleeting dreams,
I stood where Popocatapetl
    In the sunlight gleams.

I dimly heard the master's voice
    And boys far-off at play –
Chimborazo, Cotopaxi
    Had stolen me away.

I walked in a great golden dream
    To and fro from school –
Shining Popocatapetl
    The dusty streets did rule.

I walked home with a gold dark boy
    And never a word I'd say.
Chimborazo, Cotopaxi
    Had taken my speech away.

I gazed entranced upon his face
    Fairer than any flower –
O shining Popocatapetl!
    It was thy magic hour:

The houses, people, traffic seemed
    Thin fading dreams by day;
Chimborazo, Cotopaxi,
    They had stolen my soul away!

## October 15th

It's supposed to be the night of a splendid Hunter's Moon tonight, though the sky here is murky and overcast, so I expect we'll miss it. Still, the full moon is supposed by many to have strange effects on the body, sleeplessness, excitement. Incidents in psychiatric wards increase, doctors are on the alert. Apparently, writers are fluent and inspired on those days, which means I've wasted the day; I've written only a synopsis for my current book, which didn't need very much imagination. And made a cake, which does seem to have risen higher than usual.

Of course, the moon features in many poems, and one of the most beautiful is this fragment by Shelley. I find it in our dusty ancient copy of Palgrave's *Golden Treasury*, which I don't often take off the shelves, and am surprised to find how much lovely stuff there is in it. Ah well. Probably I should have written that chapter rather than made the cake…

**To The Moon – Percy Bysshe Shelley**

    Art thou pale for weariness
    Of climbing heaven, and gazing on the earth,
        Wandering companionless
    Among the stars that have a different birth –
And ever changing like a joyless eye
That finds no object worth its constancy.

## October 16th

Well, we did see the Hunter's Moon, late last night as we came out of a lovely concert of Mozart's *Requiem* given by Richard's choir. It hung pale, glowing and confident, high in the sky among a sifting of night clouds and a spatter of stars. So I returned to my *Golden Treasury* and Shelley again. I've tended to avoid Shelley, because he can be overblown and lush, and his personality rather unattractive, leaving his first wife to die, and dragging poor Mary, with her sick children, across fever-hot Italy. But when his poetry hits the spot it can be sensational, and I've found this haunting poem which I didn't really know before, a celebration of last night's music and the moon as well. And the sadness which overcomes Ariel when his work for Prospero is done.

***From* To A Lady With A Guitar – Percy Bysshe Shelley**
Ariel to Miranda- Take
This slave of music, for the sake
Of him who is the slave of thee;
And teach it all the harmony
In which thou canst, and only thou,
Make the delighted spirit glow,
Till joy denies itself again
And, too intense, is turn'd to pain.
For by permission and command
Of thine own Prince Ferdinand,
Poor Ariel sends this silent token
Of more than ever can be spoken;
Your guardian spirit, Ariel, who
From life to life must still pursue
Your happiness; for thus alone
Can Ariel ever find his own.
From Prospero's enchanted cell,
As the mighty verses tell,
To the throne of Naples he
Lit you o'er the trackless sea,
Flitting on your prow before,
Like a living meteor.
When you die, the silent Moon
In her interlunar swoon
Is not sadder in her cell

Than deserted Ariel.
When you live again on earth,
Like an unseen star of birth
Ariel guides you o'er the sea
Of life from your nativity.
Many changes have been run
Since Ferdinand and you begun
Your course of love, and Ariel still
Has tracked your steps and served your will.
Now in humbler, happier lot,
This is all remember'd not;
And now alas! the poor sprite is
Imprisoned for some fault of his
In a body like a grave;-
From you he only dares to crave,
For his service and his sorrow,
A smile today, a song tomorrow.

## October 21st

My birthday today, and though I've rather numbed by the number of years I've notched up (Can I really be 73? *Moi?*) having birthdays is better than the alternative, as I keep reminding myself. Mine is a little spoiled by the nasty flu I picked up somewhere on a Spanish train, and managed to pass on to Richard, so we've both been crawling around the house snuffling and coughing for the last week or so. And sadly, it probably means that we're going to have to miss a performance of one of our favourite operas, Purcell's *Fairy Queen* at Brecon Cathedral this evening. But I'm enjoying my present from Richard; a beautiful book of some of the watercolours of Edward Bawden. I love the English watercolourists of that period, the subdued yet crystalline colours, the sense of landscape often with a hint of mystery, and certainly of romance. I notice with pleasure that there was an exhibition of his watercolours in 1933 at the Zwemmer gallery, in which Gwyneth Lloyd Thomas suggested various poems as titles for the paintings and choosing one of these gives me a poem for today. Herbert also aims for clarity and sincerity in his verse, just as Bawden and Ravillious do in their paintings and what he writes here works for all writers, not just those writing about God, and it's something I try to follow in my own writing – avoid rhetorical clutter, always go for the direct, clear phrase, weigh your words with precision, don't use more words than you have to, don't flourish or show off, don't 'curl with metaphors', don't try to impress with your cleverness.

## Jordan (II) – George Herbert
When first my lines of heav'nly joyes made mention,
Such was their lustre, they did so excell,
That I sought out quaint words, and trim invention ;
My thoughts began to burnish, sprout, and swell,
Curling with metaphors a plain intention,
Decking the sense, as if it were to sell.

Thousands of notions in my brain did runne,
Off'ring their service, if I were not sped:
I often blotted what I had begunne;
This was not quick enough, and that was dead.
Nothing could seem too rich to clothe the sunne,
Much lesse those joyes which trample on his head.

As flames do work and winde, when they ascend,
So did I weave my self into the sense.

But while I bustled, I might heare a friend
Whisper, *How wide is all this long pretence!*
*There is in love a sweetnesse readie penn'd:*
*Copie out only that, and save expense.*

## October 24<sup>th</sup>

I thought, when I'd written my last book, the third in a trilogy about the girls who took part in the Trojan War, that it was also probably my *last* book. I thought chemo had dulled my brain, frizzled up my imagination, and even dampened my desire to write, though I'd been making up stories in my head for as long as I could remember. So no more writing, then. I tried to settle down to a life without those stories going on all the time.

But then, my publisher suggested an idea, and rather to my surprise, I found the characters were jumping up at me and demanding to be heard. This current story is about someone I initially didn't think I wanted to write about – Helen of Troy. She plays a part in two of my *Girls of Troy* series, the first, *Helen's Daughter*, where we meet Hermione, her abandoned daughter, and the second, *The Burning Towers*, where we encounter her in Troy. Was this person going to intrigue me enough? What had made her the way she was? Otherworldly beauty is the thing that set her apart from other women, and though it had its advantages, it could also be a handicap, for it made normal human interaction difficult. How did she live with this beauty? I started writing my story, with Helen telling me about herself, her feelings, her ambitions, and also her problems. Not many people know that part of her story is that she was abducted as a child by Theseus; at first I'd been rather irritated by having to incorporate this into my story, but then I realised that this would have had a permanent effect on her, on her relations with other people, with her determination not to be forced into an unpleasant relationship again. And while she could have no love for the predatory Theseus, she began to think about what love might mean, storing these thoughts up for later.

One of the greatest poems about the events that brought Helen into the world is Yeats's poem about the rape of Leda; a life begun so unnaturally must be played out in strange ways, we feel.

**Leda and the Swan – W.B. Yeats**
A sudden blow: the great wings beating still

Above the staggering girl, her thighs caressed
By the dark webs, her nape caught in his bill,
He holds her helpless breast upon his breast.

How can those terrified vague fingers push
The feathered glory from her loosening thighs?
And how can body, laid in that white rush,
But feel the strange heart beating where it lies?

A shudder in the loins engenders there
The broken wall, the burning roof and tower
And Agamemnon dead.
Being so caught up,
So mastered by the brute blood of the air,
Did she put on his knowledge with his power
Before the indifferent beak could let her drop?

## October 26th

My writer friend, Sandra Horn, with whom I've been discussing the Helen story, gave me a lovely surprise this morning, when she sent me a 'Leda' poem that she'd written, and which I like very much. There are several versions of the strange birth of Helen – Sandra looks to one which has Helen and her sister Clytemnestra both born from the same egg. I love the intensity of the mother's feelings, the sense that even though she knows the births may bring trouble, she cannot bear to destroy her own daughters.

## Leda – Sandra Horn

I carry it with me
In the warm fold between my breasts,
Cradle its round smoothness in my hands,
Close my eyes, remember
White enfolding wings, downy softness,
Then thrusting power and heat
Taking me to the very brink of death.
Leaving me not death, but life.
New life, my daughters yet-to-be.
I feel their twin hearts beating against mine.
The time is near.
Lately, I dream of blood,
I hear men screaming and the clash of arms.
Then like a whisper in my ear, the unbidden thought:
Break the egg! Smash it now!

I am their mother. I cannot.

## October 31st

Hallowe'en tonight, and the shops are full of images of nastiness; all this seems a bit unnecessary when across the other side of the Atlantic a man with a truly dark and ugly soul seems at the moment to stand a serious chance of becoming the most powerful man on earth; never have I hoped so hard for someone to lose an election.

A nicer anniversary today is Keats' birthday, and since our shopping takes us to Moorgate, where Keats was born and grew up until his father died, it's a good place to think about him, though the pub on the site where he used to live is now in the messy centre of the Crossrail excavations. Here's Keats meditating sadly about his anxieties that he'll die young before he'd had time to write all he wanted to. Death stalked his family – he was right to fear it.

### When I Have Fears That I May Cease to Be – John Keats
When I have fears that I may cease to be
    Before my pen has gleaned my teeming brain
Before high-pilèd books, in charactery
    Hold like ripe garners the full ripened grain;
When I behold, upon the night's starred face,
    Huge cloudy symbols of a high romance,
And think that I may never live to trace
    Their shadows with the magic hand of chance;
And when I feel, fair creature of an hour,
    That I shall never look upon thee more,
Never have relish in the faery power
    Of unreflecting love – then on the shore
Of the wide world I stand alone, and think
    Till love and fame to nothingness do sink.

# November

## November 9th

The nightmare is real, and the new American President embodies our darkest fears. The shock, the horror, the platitudes, the clichés have already started and won't stop for a bit.

Poetry – does it help at a time like this? I think it does – not that it can change anything, or can reach the sulphurous hearts of the Trump supporters, but a poet can tell the truth, or at least try to do so. Facebook has been full of strange beasts slouching towards Bethlehem, and the roars of departing faith. Well, for what it's worth, here's my effort

## November 9th, 2016

Why? is what the children ask;
They want to know. They need to know.
They think we know.

We do our best. We say
Because.
But know we lie.

We say Because, but soon they know
We don't know anything.
They learn our doubts, become like us,
And grow.
Each day, the news uproots us.

The world cracks,
A star drowns,
We have nowhere else to go.

## November 19th

From a world which seems to be turning nastier by the day, it's still a relief to look out of the window and see the remnants of one of the most beautiful autumns I can remember. Most of the leaves have fallen, but some are still massed in banks of deep gold, amber and bronze. It's bitterly cold, but some mornings the sky is blue and clear, and the sun paints shadows low on the hills, which are still bright summer green.

This all reminds me of Laurence Binyon's poem. In this poem, the burning leaves symbolise the terrible end of a terrible year; if only we could burn away our bad year with the leaves.

### *From* The Burning Of The Leaves – Laurence Binyon

Now is the time for the burning of the leaves.
They go to the fire; the nostril pricks with smoke
Wandering slowly into a weeping mist.
Brittle and blotched, ragged and rotten sheaves!
A flame seizes the smouldering ruin and bites
On stubborn stalks that crackle as they resist.

The last hollyhock's fallen tower is dust;
All the spices of June are a bitter reek,
All the extravagant riches spent and mean.
All burns! The reddest rose is a ghost;
Sparks whirl up, to expire in the mist: the wild
Fingers of fire are making corruption clean.

Now is the time for stripping the spirit bare,
Time for the burning of days ended and done,
Idle solace of things that have gone before:
Rootless hope and fruitless desire are there;

Let them go to the fire, with never a look behind.
The world that was ours is a world that is ours no more.

They will come again, the leaf and the flower, to arise
From squalor of rottenness into the old splendour,
And magical scents to a wondering memory bring;
The same glory, to shine upon different eyes.
Earth cares for her own ruins, naught for ours.
Nothing is certain, only the certain spring.

## November 20<sup>th</sup>

One of the things about being old and not very well and counting your remaining years is that you develop a tendency to go over the past, not always in a good way, remembering little acts of your unkindness or neglect that you hardly noticed in your busy youth but now return to look at you reproachfully. Sometimes, they're nice things you remember, and the remembrance sends little shafts of pleasure through your mind. (I recall my father, in his last years, sitting in his chair, when he thought no-one could hear him – his mind was sound, but he was very deaf, – going over and over anecdotes of his youth and love-life, reassuring himself as he went.)

Sometimes you remember insults and unkindnesses to yourself; like Shakespeare, you grieve o'er grievances forgone, which you *new pay as if not paid before*. This incident is hardly a grievance or an insult, but for some reason it's stuck. I shall call it the story of 'Martha.' Richard, being a professor at London University, brought many academic friends home over the years. With a few notable and nice exceptions, most of these people regarded me as a piece of damp wallpaper, whose shelf-full of kiddy books was not to be measured against their array of academic tomes and ground-shattering articles, whose conversation about poetry and art was not to be matched against theirs of conference papers and reputations. But this lady, who was coming to lunch, from some American university, Richard assured me was nice; warm and friendly; I would like her.

It was a Sunday morning lunch; I must have got up late anyway, the house was a tip; I think teenage daughters were still in residence, though I'm quite capable of making my own tips. Anyway, for the next couple of hours, I rushed around like a mad thing, clearing away papers and soft-drink tins and abandoned trainers, plumping up the cushions, sweeping a week's paper junk off the kitchen-dining table, getting the lunch ready (Richard isn't such a chauvinist that he'd expect me to do all the cooking – we'd shared that, but half of the meal was still a lot to prepare.) Anyway, just a few minutes before they were due to arrive, I'd got everything under control, the house looked nice, the lunch simmered away merrily. Now the only thing that was still a mess was myself. I tore upstairs, and looked frantically through the wardrobe for something that was clean and ironed. In the end, I found a grey skirt and matching sweater. I quite like grey – worn nicely, it's chic and rather French, I think. Anyway, I managed to get downstairs, still panting, before the doorbell rang, and fixed a welcoming smile to my face. Richard was right, she seemed warm and friendly, and even willing to talk to me. Before many minutes, as we sat down and started our drinks, she said that I reminded her of her friend Martha; I would like Martha. Martha, as she could see I was, was very creative. I wrote – Martha wrote too. Martha wrote so much, poetry, journals, articles; she was always having stuff published. We went downstairs, and sat at the table. Needless to say, Martha was a wonderful cook – always a tray-bake on the go, a hot-pot simmering on the stove. And what a nice kitchen we had – of course Martha was a demon at making her house pretty, rescuing furniture and making it like new, doing little friezes and decorations. Did she mention that Martha also painted? Did I paint too? Oh how nice. Martha had had an exhibition of her pictures last year.

On and on the meal went accompanied by the wonders of Martha. In fact soon it became clear to me that far from our guest thinking I was like Martha, everything I could do faded into pale comparison with what Martha did.

We finished our lunch in our pretty-but-not-quite- pretty-enough kitchen. We had our dessert, our coffee. It was time to go. Our guest was still very smiling and gracious about what a nice afternoon she'd had. But as we rose, and started to move towards the door, she stopped, leaned forward, and plucked at my grey sweater. 'You know,' she said softly, 'if *Martha* had been wearing that, she'd have tied a *bright* little scarf around the neck.'

Well, this doesn't deserve a poem. I've long forgotten the name of our guest, and I'm sure she doesn't remember that afternoon of steadily diminishing me, when I'd tried so hard to be hospitable. I expect Martha is still out there somewhere, grey-haired and gracious, wearing her handmade jewellery and her bright little scarf, sitting on her homemade cushions, penning little poems and making little sketches. And good luck to her.

## November 21st

It was a bad idea to get started on this poetry-free grudge theme. This time it was visiting an Indian couple from the University of Somewhere-or-other, and from the start she was determined to play a game of Humiliate-the-White-Woman. It started when she saw a picture of my baby. Now, there's only one thing you say when someone shows you their baby picture, and that's 'ah, how gorgeous.' But she gave a critical sniff and said she only liked babies with fat little arms, and my baby's arms were too thin. Then, when she produced the meal, she said that she'd made a special mild curry, just for me. I took a mouthful and nearly exploded. No, it wasn't mild, and she knew it. Then, the most bizarre thing of all, at the end of the meal, while we were still at the table, she brought out a pile of her sparkly Indian bangles, and insisted that I try them on. Now the only reason for this had to be to compare her dainty little Oriental wrists and hands with my big raw-boned English limbs. Still, though my hands aren't especially small or dainty, my wrists are about the smallest size there is, and so after a bit of squashing over my hand, I got the bangles on to my wrist, where they rattled about as loose as anything. Game, set and match to me, I think.

No more grudges now. And back to poetry.

## November 23rd

A grey dank day, of storms and wind and sodden leaves and muddy water pouring down the road; a suitable background to the scary world of Trump which is now emerging, a world in which the unsayable is said, the unthinkable is thought, the unimaginable is only too real; the world of post-truth.

John Donne looked for truth in the murky world of seventeenth-century religion, and in this famous passage, he shows his verbal skill in the convoluted and ragged language in which he describes the difficult quest for it, a quest Donald Trump is unlikely to take much interest in.

## *From* Satyre III – John Donne

...though truth and falsehood bee
Neare twins, yet truth a little elder is;
Be busie to seeke her, believe mee this,
Hee's not of none, nor worst, that seekes the best.
To adore, or scorne an image, or protest,
May all be bad; doubt wisely; in strange way
To stand inquiring right, is not to stray;
To sleepe, or runne wrong, is. On a huge hill
Cragged and steep, Truth stands, and hee that will
Reach her, about must and about must go;
And what the hills suddenness resists, win so;

## November 29th

Although it's been bitterly cold, the last few days have been beautiful, waking up to fields drenched in shimmering frost, rose-coloured skies, fallen red apples and yellow berries being eagerly attacked by thrushes and blackbirds. It's too cold to go out for pleasure, though, and the milder weather when it returns will be accompanied by grey skies and the usual November gloom. I'm just finishing my story of Helen of Troy, so this poem by Emma Lazarus – famous for her sonnet on the statue of Liberty – speaks to me on this November day. I shall miss Helen, though she's been a difficult companion at times. My story finishes when she's sixteen, and though I can't really forgive her for the things she's going to do in ten years' time, I try to understand what led her to the topless towers. The Cranes of the title come from a late Greek legend, and were written about in a poem by Schiller. The poet Ibycus, when attacked by robbers, called upon a flock of cranes to witness his murder. Later, the murderer implicated himself by calling out that a flock of cranes flying past were 'the cranes of Ibycus.'

**The Cranes of Ibycus – Emma Lazarus**
Here was a man who watched the river flow
Past the huge town, one grey November day.

Round him in narrow high-piled streets at play
The boys made merry as they saw him go,
Murmuring half-loud, with eyes upon the stream,
The immortal screed he held within his hand.

For he was walking in an April land
With Faust and Helen.
Shadowy as a dream
Was the prose-world, the river and the town.

Wild joy possessed him; through enchanted skies
He saw the cranes of Ibycus swoop down.

He closed the page, he lifted up his eyes,
Lo- a black line of birds in wavering thread
Bore him the greetings of the deathless dead!

# December

## December 5th

Christina Rossetti, whose birthday it is today, has a not entirely fair reputation of being a gloomy poet. But she had a sense of humour too, as this arch and teasing poem shows, a charming way of telling people to mind their own business.

**Winter – My Secret – Christina Rossetti**
I tell my secret? No indeed, not I:
Perhaps some day, who knows?
But not today; it froze and blows and snows,
And you're too curious: fie!
You want to hear it? Well:
Only my secret's mine, and I won't tell.

Or, after all, perhaps there's none:
Suppose there is no secret after all,
But only just my fun.
Today's a nipping day, a biting day,
In which one wants a shawl,
A veil, a cloak, and other wraps:
I cannot ope to everyone who taps,
And let the draughts come whistling through my hall;
Come bounding and surrounding me,
Come buffeting, astounding me,
Nipping and clipping through my wraps and all.
I wear my mask for warmth: whoever shows
His nose to Russian snows
To be pecked at by every wind that blows?

You would not peck? I thank you for good will,
Believe, but leave the truth untested still.

Spring's an expansive time: yet I don't trust
March with its peck of dust,
Nor April with its rainbow-crowned brief showers,
Not even May, whose flowers
One frost may wither through the sunless hours.

Perhaps some languid summer day,
When drowsy birds sing less and less,
And golden fruit is ripening to excess,
If there's not too much sun nor too much cloud,
And the warm wind is neither still nor loud,
Perhaps my secret I may say,
Or you may guess.

## December 12<sup>th</sup>

My copy of the Collected Poems of Hardy is a great big doorstop of a book, and I often get bogged down when I'm rifling through it, although I know there are lots of lovely Hardy poems that I haven't yet discovered. So I'm glad when other people find them for me and bring them to my attention. One of my favourite poetry blogs, *First Known When Lost,* posted this, in a piece about those brief poems, often Chinese or Japanese, that capture just a moment, so that the reader shares it and becomes part of it.

## Lying Awake – Thomas Hardy

You, Morningtide Star, now are steady-eyed, over the east,
    I know it as if I saw you:
You, Beeches, engrave on the sky your thin twigs, even the least:
    Had I paper and pencil, I'd draw you.
You, Meadow, are white with your counterpane cover of dew,
    I see it as if I were there:
You, Churchyard, are lightening faint from the shade of the yew,
    The names creeping out everywhere.

## December 19th

Winter has turned dreary – *dreich* – as the Scots put it so expressively. We travel back from London where we're been spending a few days, through grey mists creeping along the ground, colourless overcast skies, bare black trees lost in hidden distances. I'm feeling in quite good shape, having recently come back from my monthly check-up with a good report; bad guys going down, everything else pretty stable, so I'm optimistic about still being around next year.

As we get closer to Wales, the sky starts to clear a little, and streaks of blue sky appear between the clouds. Over the car radio, comes a poetry programme, and I hear a snatch of this poem by Thomas Campion, celebrating the pleasures of winter nights; though the Elizabethan winter must have been terrible to endure, with the lower temperatures of the mini-ice age, no central heating, no dry clothes, no fresh food.

In a couple of days it'll be the Winter Solstice, the shortest day, at which point Richard, who hates winter, always starts cheering up. This poem will send him on his way to spring.

## Winter Nights – Thomas Campion

Now winter nights enlarge
The number of their hours,
And clouds their storms discharge
Upon the airy towers.
Let now the chimneys blaze
And cups o'erflow with wine:
Let well-tuned words amaze
With harmony divine.
Now yellow waxen lights
Shall wait on honey love,
While youthful revels, masques and courtly sights
Sleep's leaden spells remove.

The time doth well dispense
With lover's long discourse:
Much speech hath some defence,
Though beauty no remorse.
All do not all things well:
Some measures comely tread,
Some knotted riddles tell,
Some poems smoothly read.
The summer hath his joys,
And winter his delights:
Though love and all his pleasures are but toys,
They shorten tedious nights.

## December 22nd

### Solstice

The long night over,
the year turns on its heel.
A low sun in a silver sky,
the road shines like a mirror.
Trees hold their bright berries thriftily
so birds can have their fill.
The past months are folded back into darkness,
those to come a mystery.
A flock of fieldfares lifts in a cloud;
we buy oranges and holly wreaths.
The next stop is Spring.

### Christmas Day

We wake to a muggy grey day, as one of those curiously named storms finishes its circuit around us, and to the buzzing sound of what Richard (correctly, we find later) surmises as the lads on the next hill trying out their new Christmas motorbikes. We go to church at our pretty twelfth-century church – one of a clutch of four locally dedicated to St David, and which the diocese, not appreciating that churches where people have worshipped for centuries, should be cherished and conserved, would like to replace by rational services in church halls with stacking chairs and tea-urns. We're spending Christmas on our own this year, and we return to open our remaining presents and drink white wine with Christmas snacks, to the accompaniment of Britten's *Ceremony of Carols*. Later, while Richard prepares our Christmas dinner of venison, I snuggle in a chair, wearing the lovely knitted grey jacket he's just given me (no bright little scarf around the neck, though) reading another Christmas present of Alan Bennet's diaries. I'm sure Alan Bennett would hate to be called 'cosy' but he's just right to provide a warm glow this morning, and a rest from all the horrible news still current in the world.

I find this lovely medieval carol in Britten's *Ceremony of Carols*.

## There is no Rose – Anon

There is no rose of such vertu
As is the rose that bare Jesu
*Alleluia, alleluia.*

For in this rose conteined was
Heaven and earth in litel space
*Res Miranda, res Miranda.*

By that rose we may well see
There be one God in persons three,
*Pares forma, pares forma.*

The angels sungen the shepherds to:
*Gloria in excelsis Deo,*
*Gaudeamus, gaudeamus.*

Leave we all this werldly mirth
And follow we this joyful birth,
*Transeamus, transeamus,*
*Alleluia, res Miranda,*
*Pares forma, gaudeamus,*
*Transeamus.*

## Boxing Day

Off later to a jolly lunch with friends; meanwhile, as I put away the Britten CD, I notice that on the same disk is his setting of *Rejoice In The Lamb*, that strange sad long poem by mad Christopher Smart, which also contains what must be everyone's favourite cat poem, and which makes a good celebration for Boxing Day.

### *from* Rejoice In The Lamb – Christopher Smart

For I will consider my cat Jeoffry.
For he is the servant of the living God, duly and daily serving him.
For at the first glance of the glory of God in the East he worships in his way.
For this is done by wreathing his body seven times round with elegant quickness…
…For he is of the tribe of Tiger.
For the Cherub Cat is a term of the Angel Tiger.
For he has the subtlety and hissing of a serpent, which in goodness he suppresses.
For he will not do destruction if he is well-fed, neither will he spit without provocation.
For he purrs in thankfulness when God tells him he's a good cat.
For he is an instrument for the children to learn benevolence upon.
For every house is incomplete without him, and a blessing is lacking in the spirit…
…For he knows that God is his Saviour.
For there is nothing sweeter than his peace when he is at rest…

## December 28th

The year is fast running out – would be glad to see the back of it, except there's no sign that the next will be any better. We wake to find yet another of what does seem to be an unusual number of premature celebrity deaths this year – this time Carrie Fisher, a bright and intelligent woman, and surely the only Hollywood princess worth admiring.

It's bitterly cold today – heralded by a sky of fantastic blue last night and Venus shining like a great golden lamp. This morning everything is silver-white with frost, and we decide not to go out. I'm as excited as a small boy when a big yellow helicopter flies over and around us, hovering near our garden – though less excited when a man knocks on our door and tells us they're going to have to replace the electricity pole that sits on the edge of our garden. 'Have to dig up a bit of your garden to get to it. Just going to bring a small digger in,' he says cheerfully. I hastily calculate what precious things I've got growing there; all my sage, my sorrel, my horseradish, a deep crimson William Shakespeare rose, a red dogwood…goodbye to all that, I think.

This winter day makes me remember another of Shakespeare's sonnets, number 97, the twin to 98, which I've already posted. To Shakespeare, Winter represented everything that was dark, depressing and empty; all the feelings he had when he was away from his love.

### Sonnet 97 – William Shakespeare.
How like a winter hath my absence been
From thee, the pleasure of the fleeting year!
What freezings have I felt, what dark days seen!
What old December's bareness everywhere!
And yet this time removed was summer's time;
The teeming autumn, big with rich increase,
Bearing the wanton burden of the prime,
Like widow'd wombs after their lord's decease;

Yet this abundant issue seem'd to me
But hope of orphans and unfather'd fruit;
For summer and his pleasures wait on thee,
And thou away, the very birds are mute;
    Or if they sing, 'tis with so dull a cheer,
    That leaves look pale, dreading the winter's near.

## December 31st

Well, the last day of the year, and a year that very few people will feel sentimental about; too much war, too many terrorist murders, too many sad refugees, and to crown everything, Donald Trump, striding around like one of the madder Roman emperors. And worst still, it's impossible to feel optimistic about 2017, in which all the horrors of 2016 seem on course to be re-enacted.

    Still, for ourselves, it hasn't been too bad a year. I'm still here, for a start, and though I'm not in perfect health, am in better shape than I was this time last year, and feel hopeful that I'm going to be able to manage the next year at least. We've done some travelling, been to Spain, seen Las Meninas and the Sagrada Familia, had a lovely Welsh holiday with all our family, I've written a book, we're planning a trip to Vienna where Richard is attending a conference in the spring, and thinking about another holiday later. Amsterdam? I'm going through a Van Gogh moment, and would love to see as many as I can of his paintings, with their miraculous swirling brushstrokes and dazzling colours. Or maybe Rome, or Berlin… anyway choosing will give us much pleasure. Our family, and especially our grandchildren continue to be a delight – having grandchildren feels like being awarded an unexpected prize, just when you thought all the days of prizes were over. I'm only sorry that not being the strong and active woman I was a few years ago, I can't see as much of them as I'd like or do as many things with them.

What poem to choose? Most end of year poems are a bit melancholy (*The year is dying, let it die,* says Tennyson) and while that might suit this particular year, I'd like to end on something upbeat. So I find this lovely poem by Yeats; it's new to me, and not in my Collected Poems, so I imagine he must have discarded it, but I like it, and it suits a writer, wondering about the point of all those words. Goodbye, 2016, goodbye this diary. What's to come is still unsure…

**Where My Books Go – W.B. Yeats**
All the words that I utter,
And all the words that I write
Must spread out their wings untiring,
And never rest in their flight,
Till they come where your sad, sad heart is,
And sing to you in the night
Beyond where the waters are moving,
Storm-darken'd or starry bright.

# Acknowledgements

I should like to acknowledge the following copyrights and permissions:

Norman Nicholson – The Undiscovered Planet, published by Faber and Faber, published by permission of David Higham Associates.

The extract from Reynard The Fox – John Masefield is printed by kind permission of The Society of Authors as the Literary Representative of the Estate of John Masfield.

Weathermaps – © 2016 Jane Stemp. All rights reserved

Leda ©2016 Sandra Horn. All rights reserved

Blackbird, The Day the Sun came out, Evening, Seasonal, November 9th 2017, Butterflies at Sea, Las Meninas, Dead Bullfinch, Solstice ©2016 Frances Thomas. All rights reserved.

Moral Rights have been asserted for all authors.

I have made every attempt to trace copyrights, but if I have omitted any, please get in touch with me and I will rectify the matter.

Copyright, though I approve of it entirely, can be a difficult beast. I regret having to omit W.H. Auden's poem 'Look, Stranger' simply because his American agents have not replied to my application for permission and my polite reminder. The poem of course can be found on Google where thousands of poems mill around without any copyright.

I'd like to thank all the friends who have been so helpful and enthusiastic about this book; Jane Stemp, Sandra Horn, Philip Bowen and Sue Best, Tony and Sarah Thomas, Colin and Sarah

Tucker, Barbara Nash and Jemma Smy and of course Richard who has coped cheerfully with this rather dreary year of hospital visits. My lovely family, Harriet, Lucy, Matt, Lily and Jacob have made the year far less gloomy than it might have been. And the nurses and consultants at the Macmillan Renton Unit in Hereford have kept me alive to enjoy it.

# Index of poems and poets

| | | |
|---|---|---|
| Anon | *Alysoun* | 45 |
| | from *Beowulf* | 86 |
| | *Panguar Ban* | 62 |
| | *Rose Cheek'd Laura* | 25 |
| | *Sumer is ycumin in* | 161 |
| | *There is no Rose* | 204 |
| Matthew Arnold | from *Poor Matthias* | 107 |
| William Barnes | *Linden Lea* | 103 |
| Laurence Binyon | *The Burning of the Leaves* | 192 |
| | *The Winds of All the World* | 51 |
| William Blake | from *Auguries of Innocence* | 60 |
| Robert Bridges | *A Passer-By* | 81 |
| Elizabeth Barratt Browning | from *Aurora Leigh* | 55 |
| Robert Burns | *Ae Fond Kiss* | 13 |
| | *John Anderson, my Jo* | 164 |
| Lord Byron | *Ah Gentle Fleeting…* | 39 |
| Thomas Campion | *Winter Nights* | 202 |
| C.P. Cavafy | *Ithaka* | 134 |
| John Clare | from *The Shepherd's Calendar* | 115 |
| | " " | 117 |
| William J. Cory | *Heraclitus* | 98 |
| William Cowper | *Epitaph on a Hare* | 110 |
| George Crabbe | from *Peter Grimes* | 83 |
| Richard Crashaw | *The Flaming Heart* | 132 |
| W.H. Davies | *April's Charms* | 79 |
| | *Rich Days* | 175 |

| | | |
|---|---|---|
| Emily Dickinson | *I Died For Beauty* | 83 |
| | *Because I Could Not Stop* | 92 |
| John Donne | *Good Friday* | 72 |
| | from *Satyre III* | 197 |
| Ernest Dowson | *A Last Word* | 138 |
| | *They Are Not Long* | 161 |
| John Drinkwater | *Moonlit Apples* | 176 |
| John Dryden | *After The Great Fire* | 172 |
| William Dunbar | *Sweet Rose Of Virtue* | 106 |
| Rachel Field | *If Once You Have Slept on an Island* | 163 |
| James Elroy Flecker | *The Golden Road to Samarkand* | 136 |
| Emperor Hadrian | *Animula Vagula Blanda* | 38 |
| Thomas Hardy | *Between Us Now* | 151 |
| | *Lying Awake* | 201 |
| | *The Roman Road* | 169 |
| | *An Unkindly May* | 95 |
| | *The Year's Awakening* | 17 |
| Felicia Hemans | *The Hour of Death* | 68 |
| George Herbert | *The Flower* | 139 |
| | *Jordan II* | 186 |
| | *Prayer* | 162 |
| | *Redemption* | 43 |
| Robert Herrick | *Dreams* | 43 |
| Gerard Manly Hopkins | *Sonnet 41* | 151 |
| | *Spring* | 57 |
| Sandra Horn | *Leda* | 189 |
| A.E. Housman | from *More Poems VII* | 162 |
| | *A Shropshire Lad XXXI* | 142 |

| | | |
|---|---|---|
| Dr Samuel Johnson | *Oh Long Soul* | 39 |
| Ben Jonson | *Slow Slow Fresh Fount* | 78 |
| | *To The Memory…* | 90 |
| John Keats | *Ode to Autumn* | 174 |
| | *When I Have Fears* | 190 |
| Rudyard Kipling | *Justice* | 119 |
| D.H. Lawrence | *Bavarian Gentians* | 58 |
| Emma Lazarus | *The Cranes of Ibycus* | 198 |
| John Lloyd | from *Thoughts of Boyhood* | 50 |
| Amy Lowell | *Meeting House Hill* | 35 |
| Christopher Marlowe | from *Dr Faustus* | 53 |
| Andrew Marvell | *The Garden* | 127 |
| John Masefield | from *Reynard The Fox* | 20 |
| Alice Meynell | *November Blue* | 40 |
| Charlotte Mew | *I So Liked Spring* | 70 |
| John Milton | from *Paradise Lost* | 108 |
| William Vaughan Moody | *A Grey Day* | 37 |
| Edith Nesbit | *Baby Seed Song* | 19 |
| Norman Nicholson | *The Undiscovered Planet* | 12 |
| Alexander Pope | *Ah Fleeting Spirit* | 38 |
| Rainer Maria Rilke | *The Last Supper* | 71 |
| Isaac Rosenberg | *August 1914* | 146 |
| Christina Rossetti | *Another Spring* | 94 |
| | *At Last* | 21 |
| | from *Goblin Market* | 157 |
| | *Soul, Rudderless, Unbraced* | 39 |
| | *Spring* | 64 |
| | *Winter, My Secret* | 199 |

| | | |
|---|---|---|
| William Shakespeare | Fear No More | 27 |
| | from Romeo and Juliet | 67 |
| | " " | 97 |
| | from Midsummer Night's Dream | 36 |
| | from Sir Thomas More | 16 |
| | Sonnet 30 | 33 |
| | Sonnet 97 | 206 |
| | Sonnet 98 | 80 |
| Percy Bysshe Shelley | from Adonais | 44 |
| | To The Moon | 183 |
| | from Lady With a Guitar | 184 |
| Sir Philip Sidney | from Solitariness | 159 |
| William Soutar | The Permanence of the Young Men | 105 |
| | In The Time of Tyrants | 162 |
| Christopher Smart | from Rejoice in the Lamb | 205 |
| Jane Stemp | Weather Maps | 124 |
| Robert Louis Stephenson | When I was down | 166 |
| Sarah Teasdale | There will come soft rains | 34 |
| Alfred Lord Tennyson | In Memoriam CXIV | 41 |
| Sir Thomas Wyatt | Whoso List His Wealth | 30 |
| Edward Thomas | Rain | 11 |
| | March | 76 |
| | In Memoriam | 130 |
| James Thomson | The Wine of Love | 121 |
| Thomas Traherne | Fullness | 32 |
| | Wonder | 147 |
| W.J. Turner | Romance | 181 |
| Henry Vaughan | My soul, my pleasant soul... | 38 |
| | Retirement | 156 |

| | | |
|---|---|---|
| William Wordworth | *Lines Composed a Few Miles Above Tintern Abbey* | 89 |
| William Butler Yeats | *Leda and the Swan* | 188 |
| | *The Wild Swans of Coole* | 23 |
| | *When you are Old* | 31 |
| | *The Withering of the Boughs* | 122 |

www.ingramcontent.com/pod-product-compliance
Lightning Source LLC
Chambersburg PA
CBHW070145100426
42743CB00013B/2818